RUNNING AMOK

RUNNING AMOK:

An Historical Inquiry

by

John C. Spores

Ohio University Center for International Studies
Monographs in International Studies

Southeast Asia Series Number 82
Athens, Ohio 1988

Library of Congress Cataloging-in-Publication Data

Spores, John C.
    Running amok : an historical inquiry / John C. Spores.
        p.   cm. -- (Monographs in international studies. Southeast
Asia series : no. 82)
    Bibliography: p.
    ISBN 0-89680-140-3 (pbk.) :
    1.Psychoses--Malaya--History.   2. Homicide--Malaya--Psychological
aspects--History.   3. Cultural psychiatry.   I. Ohio University. Center
for Southeast Asian Studies. II. Title. III. Series.
RC512.S66   1988
362.2--dc19   88-5253
                                             CIP

ISBN 0-89680-140-3

CONTENTS

To Gayl Ness and Henry Meyer.
Your guidance and scholarly
example are deeply appreciated.

ACKNOWLEDGEMENTS

A detailed study of running amok as a topic through which doctoral studies in sociology, social work, and Southeast Asian Studies might be integrated was originally the creative suggestion of Gayl Ness. Professor Ness and Henry Meyer of the University of Michigan were both instrumental in guiding the course of the study, originally developed as a doctoral dissertation, and in offering support and encouragement where needed. I particularly thank them for their flexibility in fostering a project outside the normal mold and for their patience during a prolonged period of research and analysis. The topic proved ideal and has held my interest for many years.

This investigation has required review of a multitude of historical sources and my respect is great for those individuals, past and present, bearing responsibility for building the fine collections at the University of Michigan, the United States Library of Congress, and the New York City Public Library. The historian can certainly identify with the excitement one experiences in discovering in some obscure volume lying untouched for decades that bit of data offering new insights and guiding the analysis on a more certain course. Those who see that the sources are available have my gratitude.

Admiration and respect are also due those European chroniclers of travels, events, and experiences in Southeast Asia and India. Without these accounts this investigation would be impossible or at least require a radically altered form. The works of Raffles, Clifford, Swettenham, and Winstedt have been of particular value.

Manuscript revision has been aided substantially by the comments and suggestions offered by an individual, unknown to me, who initially reviewed the manuscript for the Ohio University Center for International studies. The reviewer was thorough and insightful, leading to numerous improvements in the final version. Additionally, editorial staff

ix

for the Monographs in International Studies series are to be thanked for their skills in making the analysis far more readable.

A number of individuals aided my efforts, in one way or another, and their contributions are acknowledged gratefully. Among them: Aminudin Haji Sulaiman, Amran Halim, Barbara Watson Andaya, Stanley Bedlington, Walter Connor, Irwin Epstein, Peter Gosling, Joseph Hartog, Robert McKinley, John Musgrave, Alfred Smith, Siti Hayati Abdullah, Ronald Spores, Alfred Stamm, Wazir Jahan Karim, and Aram Yengoyan. A National Defense Foreign Language fellowship made feasible my participation in the Southeast Asian Studies Program at the University of Michigan, and this major source of support is also acknowledged gratefully.

Finally, my heartfelt thanks go to Deanna, Julie, and Jennifer for sacrifices made affording me the luxury of pursuing that which is of personal interest and meaning.

Chapter 1

INTRODUCTION

The influence of culture and social organization on the forms, symptoms and incidence of mental disorder and aberrant behavior has long been recognized, and the psychogenic and sociogenic experiential bases for many such behaviors are well established within the traditions of social and transcultural psychiatry. There are so many excellent texts available in this broad field of inquiry that it is unnecessary to review its origins, history and legitimacy here.[1] However the reviews of past work by Lin and by Wittkower deserve special mention by virtue of their concern with Asian cultures.[2] It is within this tradition of the cross-cultural study of mental disorder that I undertake this analysis of the curious pattern of amok.

Amok is a Malay word with a behavioral referent that at one time provided for many Westerners their most vivid imagery of the Malay world. Included in this imagery was the visualization of a primitive Malay suddenly seizing dagger or spear and embarking on a murderous rampage, or "running amuck" as the English corruption had it. The occurrence of amok so caught the attention of early Western travelers to what is present-day Malaysia and Indonesia that British and Dutch colonialists alike frequently mentioned the practice. To read one of the more detailed descriptive accounts by a British colonial officer is perhaps the best introduction to amok.

The Amok of Imam Mamat[3]

NO. 117--REPORT OF A CASE OF AMOK, PULAU TIGA, LOWER PERAK. TO THE SECRETARY TO GOVERNMENT, TAIPING.

SIR,--With reference to the recent "amok" case at Pulau Tiga, I have the

1

honour to submit the following report for your information.

On Thursday . . . I received a letter from the Penghulu of Pulau Tiga stating that . . . the previous evening one Imam Mamat had run "amok" at Pasir Garam, killing four persons and wounding four others, and that the culprit was still at large. . . . At 8:15 a.m. we left in the police pinnace, towing one boat, to Bandar, and, with a double crew poling, reached Pasir Salak at 2:15 p.m., where we stopped for lunch whilst the Penghulu procured us a fresh crew, after which we crossed over the river to Kampong Gajah, landed, and walked overland to Pulau Tiga, reaching the "balei" after a very sharp walk at 4:30 p.m. Here we met many armed Malays returning from an unsuccessful search for the "amoker." After a few minutes rest, we again started off up stream, and crossed over to the left bank near the Lambau boundary, where we met the Penghulu, who reported the death of four adults, and one child and four others wounded. Penghulu Alang Amat, assisted by Penghulu Haji Mahomed, of Lambau, with some 200 followers, all armed with not less than three weapons apiece, had been in search of the murderer all day, but without success. We at once proceeded to the house of Bilal Abu, only to view a most ghastly scene, the walls, floor, and mats being covered with blood, and one male adult named Bilal Abu with two adult females, Alang Resak and Ngah Intan, also a little child, Teh, lay dead in the house. From the evidence, it appears Imam Mamat, who lived a little inland from Bilal Abu's (his brother-in-law) house, had been at work fencing his land all day, and about 4 to 5 p.m. he entered the house of Bilal Abu with a spear and a "golok" in his possession. On entering he took the hand of Bilal Abu and asked for pardon; he then shook hands with his wife Alang Resak and said the same thing, but immediately stabbed her in the abdomen

2

with the "golok." She immediately fell,
and received two more superficial
wounds. . . . Bilal Abu rushed to the
rescue, and received for his trouble a
deep puncture wound in the region of the
heart and a superficial wound on the
right side: he fell never to rise again.
At this moment Ngah Intan, wife of Bilal
Abu, followed by four of her children,
rushed to the door and jumped out, her
eldest boy Kassim receiving a stab in
the back as he jumped out. Imam Mamat
jumped out, and, with two more spears
picked up in the house, gave chase to
Ngah Intan, who was followed by the
three youngest children, the fourth (the
already wounded one) going in an opposite direction, but on seeing Mamat
going after his mother, he turned to
look and saw him catch up the three
children and make sundry thrusts at them
with the spears in each hand. One
little girl, Si Teh, received two wounds
in the back, not dangerous ones; a boy,
Mumin, received a deep wound in the
side, . . . his recovery being doubtful
[he subsequently died]; and the second
little girl, Si Puteh, received a severe
wound in the stomach, from which she
died the next day. Having satisfied
himself with the children, he followed
up the mother, catching her up 100 yards
off, and killed her on the spot by a
stab in the abdomen. . . . It appears
the Imam then walked down stream some
200 yards, and met a friend, Uda Majid,
who was coming up to stop him, but
unarmed. Uda Majid, saluted him
respectfully, and asked him if he
recognized him, and not to make a row;
he replied "Yes, but my spear doesn't
know you," and immediately stabbed him
twice in the breast and stomach. Uda
Majid wrested the spear from him, but
before he could do anything received a
stab in the left lung and another in the
windpipe, upon which he fell. One Ma
Adi . . . rushed unarmed to his assistance. Mamat immediately turned to stab
him, but he fled, followed a little way
by Mamat, during which Udah Majid got up

and was staggering away when Mamat returned and chased him, giving him two more wounds in the back, whereupon he fell dead. This man had six wounds in all, of which three were fatal ones. When the row first commenced it appears one Mat Sah ran up the steps of Bilal Abu's to stop Mamat, but the latter rushed at him, and on turning to flee he received a superficial wound in the back, and fell headlong to the ground; fortunately he was not followed. After the death of Uda Majid the Imam appears to have rushed off up stream along the river bank carrying three spears and a "golok." He was seen twice to wade far out into the river and then back to land. The news by this time had spread up and down, so every one was prepared. He made for a relation's house, to which his own five children, on hearing the row, had run for refuge, but when some distance off was warned off by the owner. From this point he appears to have made inland, and was not seen again.

From the evidence . . . it appears [the next evening] the "amoker" appeared opposite the house of Ngah Lassam. Fortunately the door was slammed in his face and secured. Ngah Lassam asked him what he wanted, and he said to sleep there, to which Lassam replied "Very well, but throw away your arms," in reply to which Mamat made a smart thrust through the window at Lassam, who grabbed the spear, and, with the assistance of his son, wrested the weapon from him, but at the same time received a stab in the face from a "kris" Mamat had, and before anything further could be done Mamat had partly got in at the window, whereupon Ngah Lassam seized his own spear and stabbed him in the thigh. The spear-head broke off in the wound, the "batang" falling on the floor of the house, whilst Mamat fell to the ground. In this house there were four adult males, five adult females, and seven children, their only weapon being a

4

spear. It being very dark, and not knowing what the wounded man was up to, two of the men in the house got out at the back and ran up stream some 1½ miles and called the Wakil Penghulu, giving the alarm all the way, and about 7 p.m. they returned with him. Entering the house at the back, they cautiously opened the door, and, seeing in the dim light the Imam lying there, procured a torch, with which they could see a "kris" some six feet away from Mamat on the left, and the spear-head a few feet away on the right side. Seeing this the Wakil Penghulu pounced on him and secured him, at once sending for Inspector Evans, who arrived about 9 p.m., and took him over, washing and bandaging up his wound, and removed him by stretcher and boat to the Penghulu's, where he received food and nourishment. Being unable to procure a good-sized boat, Mr. Evans was unable to leave for Teluk Anson till 7 a.m. next morning, arriving at 3:30 p.m. The wounded man, who had been vomiting incessantly since his capture, was at once conveyed to hospital and properly attended to, but succumbed to his injuries at 8 p.m. . . .

The District Surgeon arriving next morning, held a post mortem. . . . I held an inquest, and returned a verdict in accordance with the medical evidence, at the same time justifying the action of Ngah Lassam, to whom great credit is due. The Penghulu of Pulau Tiga, Alang Amat, the Penghulu of Lambau, Haji Mahomed, and Anjang Talih, Wakil Penghulu Lambau Kiri, deserve the thanks of Government for the prompt action they took and the assistance rendered. There was no reason whatever for this "amoker's" action, he being on most friendly terms with every one, and he himself said he did not know what he was doing, only his head went round and the devil told him to do it. He also stated he had been living on remnants of food, etc., . . . that he heard the people

5

searching for him, also that he had hidden two of the spears near the scene of the murder, and pointed out the spot as the boat came down stream, and on landing Inspector Evans found the spears. The one is a short-handled, short-headed diamond-shaped spear, a very handy weapon, and the other also a short-handled narrow-bladed spear. I omitted to mention that the two females, wives of Bilal Abu and Imam Mamat, were in an advanced stage of pregnancy, . . . thus to date there are really [eight] victims. I attach a list of the killed and wounded. . . .

> J. W. Brewster,
> Assistant Superintendent
> Lower Perak

Teluk Anson, 17th February 1891

Killed--	age
Alang Resak, wife of Imam Mamat	33
Bilau Abu, brother-in-law of "	35
Ngah Intan, wife of Bilau Abu	32
Si Puteh, daughter of "	4
Mumin, son of Bilau Abu	7
Uda Majid, Bin Chu Masseh	35

Wounded--	
Si Teh, daughter of Bilau Abu	7
Kassim, son of Bilau Abu	14
Mat Sah (Orang Kedah)	45
Ngah Lassam, of Lambau	

Areas of Inquiry

This graphic description of the amok of Imam Mamat portrays an episode of aberrant behavior that until at least the beginning of the twentieth century occurred with relative frequency among Malay peoples. The notoriety and attention the practice received led to amok becoming one of the few Malay words approaching common usage among English-speaking people.

With the passage of time, Westerners and most Malays have come to utilize the term to refer to frenzied maniacal behavior in general, often including the connotation that the behavior results in injury or damage to persons or physical objects. But in the nineteenth century the word was often used more as noun than as adjective with the referent being an episode of behavior marked by a set of relatively specific defining characteristics. Historically, amok represents a behavioral constellation unique to the Malay context and distinguishable from similar patterns occurring in other cultures. It is a culture-specific syndrome wherein an individual unpredictably and without warning manifests mass, indiscriminate, homicidal behavior that is authored with suicidal intent. Curiously, this frightful act of violence is marked by an element of cultural sanction and legitimacy. Further, there is evidence to indicate that over time the frequency of amok greatly decreased. Can explanations of these facts be developed? Can the origins of the practice be traced? What is there in the Malay cultural and historical context that could aid in accounting for the existence of amok? What were its defining characteristics and how frequently did it occur? Did amok disappear? If so, why? How have others attempted to explain the existence of this practice? These are the primary questions addressed by this intensive case study of an intriguing form of culture-specific aberrant behavior.

Background

The comparative study of mental disorder and aberrant behavior has yielded a number of patterns which might be categorized broadly as culture-bound aggressive reactions. Historically, the furor of the ancient Scandinavian practice of <u>Berserksgang</u> is well-known.[4] Other forms of aggressive reaction were reported among Turks, Sarawak Moslems, Blackfoot and Assiniboine Indians, the Bataks of Sumatra, the Indian tribes of Guiana and Northern Brazil, and other tribes in Tierra del Fuego.[5] Burton-Bradley finds that cases marked by the cardinal symptoms of amok have been reported from Trinidad, India, Liberia and elsewhere in Africa, Siberia, Polynesia and Europe.[6] Such cases also occur in the Philippines and America.[7] Burton-Bradley describes seven cases of amok from the early 1960s in Papua New Guinea and present-day Irian Jaya and notes its superficial similarity to three other patterns recently reported from this area: the "wild man behavior" among the Gururumba described by Newman, the behavior of the male in the "collective

7

hysteria" described by Reay, and the hysterical psychosis among the Bena Bena described by Langness.[8]

Certainly, present-day as well as historical reactions more or less similar to amok are to be found for many, if not most, cultures. Recent discussions of amok have come from the field of transcultural psychiatry and have concentrated on psychopathological elements of modern variants of the pattern. These discussions have generally centered on identification of common features and appropriate diagnostic classifications.[9] However, amok among the Malays of British Malaya and in what was the Netherlands East Indies, while outwardly similar in some respects to many other aggressive reaction patterns, was distinctive in its genesis, its total symptomalogical constellation, and in the manner in which it was manifested.

Methodology

As my initial investigation began to reveal the decreased frequency of amok behavior among Malays over time as well as the existence of martial antecedents with links to solitary amok, it became apparent that many of the most interesting questions relating to this topic would be best addressed by an historical inquiry.[10] This appeared particularly to be the case with respect to developing explanations for the origins of solitary amok among Malays, its apparent cultural legitimization, and its substantially decreased rate of occurrence by the first quarter of the twentieth century.

While the data and method are historical, the primary objective of this research is to add to the sociological study of sociogenic and psychogenic-based aberrant behavior, behavior driven by social and psychological rather than organic forces. Cultural, political, and economic factors are particularly emphasized within an historical framework, for the available evidence indicates that the manifestation of amok behavior changed over time in Malay societies, and such change is best understood through relating it to the unfolding of institutional spheres in these societies.

The approach employed here reflects the renewed interest of sociologists in historical analysis as a corrective to the shortcomings of structural-functional analysis for addressing social change and conflict. Certainly, structural-functional relations and their relationships to amok

8

are identified and described, but the emphasis is on how and why these relationships changed over time in ways that are significant for the form and incidence of amok. Historical analysis enables penetration of past social structures and helps to illuminate our understanding of the genesis and development of this particular pattern of behavior.

The primary data utilized are the many contemporary descriptions of amok in the eighteenth, nineteenth, and early twentieth century literature on Malaysia and Indonesia. Often these are only references in passing, and only occasionally were serious efforts made to account for the occurrence of amok. Past efforts to account for the pattern have been either incorrect or incomplete, and a more comprehensive explanation than has existed heretofore is offered in chapters four, five, and six.

This study is based almost entirely on materials located in the Harlan Hatcher Graduate Library and the Medical Library at the University of Michigan, the United States Library of Congress, and the New York Public Library.[11] The University of Michigan libraries are the primary source, and my search of the Michigan collections has been comprehensive. It is possible that useful data remain undiscovered in the other libraries as well as in repositories located elsewhere, particularly in Great Britain, the Netherlands, Malaysia, and Indonesia. Coverage of English language sources has been more thorough than that for materials written in other languages. Still a number of non-English sources were consulted and, with the possible exception of Dutch materials, it appears likely that nothing has been published in other languages which would lead to substantial alteration in this analysis. Although a number of Dutch language sources were consulted, extended search and analysis was not feasible. Because of this, the findings and generalizations in this study may hold more validity for the Peninsular Malaysian context than for Indonesia. Dutch colonial records especially need to be searched more fully.

Published materials that appeared to bear on the analysis in any way have been studied and an effort was made to view all materials known to include descriptions, analyses or references to amok. The vast majority of these sources were obtained and are taken into account. Significant additions to the pool of historical data seem unlikely--at least for the Malaysian case.

Organization of the Analysis

With this brief introduction, we now turn to the analysis proper. Chapter two identifies patterns of martial amok and contrasts their occurrence in the contexts of southern India and Malaya. This comparison suggests that patterns of martial amok provided the quasi-legitimacy accorded solitary amok in Malay cultures. The aura of heroicism surrounding martial amok is postulated as carrying over into Malay life generally. Chapter three presents a chronological review of recorded references to solitary forms of amok, providing an historical backdrop for more intensive analysis of the practice. Six detailed descriptions of solitary amok episodes are recorded as they were originally presented in the literature. Chapter four addresses more specifically the characteristics of the solitary amok episode, providing description and preliminary analysis of the various phases of such episodes, including societal reactions to amok. Finally trends in rates of incidence are discussed.

Chapter five includes a review and assessment of etiological factors cited by past observers in attempting to explain the occurrence of solitary amok. A crucial classificatory distinction is then developed between two basic categories of solitary amok. One category includes those cases which are spontaneous and without apparent motivation (Spontaneous-Unmotivated). The onset of the episode has a physiological genesis while the behaviors exhibited are culturally determined. The second category includes those cases that are motivated and intentional (Reactive-Motivated). This type of amok is reactive and aimed at restoring or avenging the loss of personal dignity suffered as a result of insult or misfortune. This categorization makes more intelligible the etiology of solitary amok while providing a basis from which to explain a longitudinal decline in the rate of incidence.

Chapter six discusses how the intensified European colonial impact on Malaya and the Netherlands East Indies toward the end of the nineteenth and at the beginning of the twentieth century engendered changes in the traditional Malay social context. Attention is directed to how such changes led to the near disappearance of amok except in a few isolated areas experiencing little Western penetration. Chapter seven summarizes the findings of the analysis and suggests areas for further investigation.

Chapter 2

MARTIAL AMOK: SOUTH INDIAN
AND MALAYSIAN CHRONOLOGIES

A chronological review of references to amok
in various written sources yields an array of
meanings and variations in behavior associated with
this term.[1] Such a review provides clues to the
origins of the Malayan and Indonesian practice as
well as a basic body of data from which to draw
explanatory inferences. While antedated by several
references to amok in the Malay world, the majority
of early references to amok-like behavior come from
sixteenth and seventeenth century southern India.
It is quite possible, as Yule and Burnell suggest,
that the term and perhaps the practice have an
Indian rather than Malay origin.[2]

There is substantial evidence of contact of
very long standing between southern India and the
Malay world. The shipping trade between Malay
regions and India, the Middle East, and Europe
occasioned much interpenetration of influences among
these regions. For instance, Islam probably came to
the Malays via southern India rather than directly
from the Middle East.[3] While a direct connection
between amok behavior in the two geographic settings
cannot be firmly established, there is certainly
circumstantial evidence to suggest that there may
have been common origins. Although Yule and Burnell
(1903) have noted similarities between amok-like
practices in India and the Malay world, no
systematic comparison has ever been made.[4]

Martial Amok in India

The passages which follow are largely from the
journals of various expeditions, and they describe
institutionalized, sometimes ritualistic behavior
patterns, often collective in nature and often
occurring in a martial context. Yule and Burnell
cite this passage from the Portuguese Gaspar Correa
written between 1512 and 1561:

11

In war between the Kings of Calicut and
Cochin (1503) two princes of Cochin were
killed. A number of these desperadoes
who have been spoken of . . . were
killed. . . . But some remained who were
not killed, and these went in shame, not
to have died avenging their lords . . .
these were more than 200, whc all,
according to their custom, shaved off
all their hair, even to the eyebrows,
and embraced each other and their
friends and relations, as men about to
suffer death. In this case they are as
madmen--known as <u>amoucos</u>--and count
themselves as already among the dead.
These men dispersed, seeking wherever
they might find men of Calicut, and
among these they rushed fearless, killing and slaying till they were slain.
And some of them, about twenty, reckon-
ing more highly of their honour, desired
to turn their death to better account;
and these separated, and found their way
secretly to Calicut, determined to slay
the king. But as it became known that
they were amoucos, the city gave the
alarm, and the King sent his servants to
slay them as they slew others. But they
like desperate men played the devil
. . . before they were slain, and killed
many people, with women and children.[5]

Of particular interest in this passage and
others relating to India is the fact that Indian
versions of amok generally include an element of
discrimination in the determination of victims. As
we shall see, discrimination in the selection of
victims is at least partially, often totally, absent
in cases of solitary amok among Malays. In this
passage too we are informed that failure of the
amoucos to be killed at the scene of battle in such
circumstances is reason for engagement in ritual
that builds and solidifies resolve to carry on a
futile battle and assure a death that erases or at
least diminishes the sense of dishonor. It should
be noted that the ritual participation does not
precede the initial occurrence of amok behavior in
battle but rather follows upon the sense of shame
that attaches to having failed to bring this
behavior to a satisfactory denouement.

William Logan, writing in 1881, provides information regarding the possible origins of the amoucos:

> Among other strange Malayali customs . . . if a chieftain was slain, his followers attacked and obstinately persevered in ravaging the slayer's country and killing his people till their vengeance was satisfied. This custom is doubtless that which was described so long ago as in the ninth century A.D. by two Muhammadans . . .: "There are kings who, upon their accession, observe the following ceremony." A quantity of cooked rice was spread before the king, and some three or four hundred persons came of their own accord and received each a small quantity of rice from the king's own hands after he himself had eaten some. "By eating of this rice they all engage to burn themselves on the day the king does, or is slain, and they punctually fulfill their promise." Men who devoted themselves to certain death on great occasions were termed "Amoucos" by the Portuguese. . . .[6]

It probably is impossible to discover if the origins of the amoucos described by Correa actually lie in the rice-eating or similar ritualistic oath-taking ceremonies of Indian antiquity. However, it is apparent that traditional supports exist in at least some parts of India legitimizing and encouraging ultimate self-sacrificial behavior. The practice of <u>suttee</u>, or widow-burning, probably flows from such traditions.[7]

In 1566, Frederike states: "The King of Cochin . . . hath a great number of gentlemen which he calleth Amocchi . . . .: these . . . men esteem not their lives anything, so that it may be for the honour of their King."[8] In 1584, Sassetti writes:

> Their forces [in Cochin] consist of a kind of soldiers whom they call amocchi, who are under obligation to die at the King's pleasure, and all soldiers who in war lose their King or their general lie under this obligation. And of such the

13

King makes use in urgent cases, sending them to die fighting.[9]

It seems evident in the Indian setting that the amocchi were first and foremost defined by their relationship to martial organizational structures and it was probably within a military context that the vast majority of their acts of frenzied homicidal-suicidal behavior occurred. However, it seems reasonable to conclude that such acts spilled over into civilian life, whether occurring as non-martial acts by one or several of the amocchi or as the acts of civilians simply running amok, perhaps in emulation of the amocchi.

One seventeenth century chronicler, Diogo de Couto, uses the term amoucos in reference to the actions of the Javanese as well as the inhabitants of the Malabar coast of southeast India. First, with regard to the Javanese:

> They are chivalrous men and of such determination that for whatever offence may be offered them they make themselves amoucos in order to get satisfaction thereof. And were a spear run into the stomach of such an one he would still press forward without fear till he got at his foe.[10]

Speaking of the amoucos of Malabar, he describes how, on the death of their king in action with the Portuguese, "nearly 4,000 Nairs [Nayar warrior caste] made themselves amoucos with the usual ceremonies, shaving their heads on one side, and swearing by their pagoda to avenge the King's death."[11]

The differences in Couto's description of the Javanese and Indian amoucos are interesting: the Javanese variety apparently consisted of affronted individuals acting alone, while the Indian variety is described as occurring in the context of the organized martial collective. The Indian reference is also noteworthy in its depiction of the existence of a ritual ceremony accompanying transition to the amoucos status as well as in its implication that the large amoucos force was not an ongoing entity but was brought into existence suddenly in reaction to the death of a king. Thus, ordinarily there may have been a relatively small amoucos contingent, the size of the force swelling only in dire circumstances. Finally, Couto provides a measure of

14

confirmation for Correa's description of ritual engagement occurring _after_ the dreaded event, the death of the king and the failure to find death on his behalf. Thus, once again there appears to be support for the idea that the ritual participatory aspect of the martial amok complex occurred only in the extreme circumstance, at a moment in a sequence of events when there remained not the least question about the desirability of self-sacrificial behavior.

In 1624, Pietro della Valle writes:

> When two Kings happen to war together each Army takes great heed not to kill the opposing King, nor so much as to strike his Umbrella wherever it goes, which is amongst them the Ensign of Royalty, because, besides that it would be a great sin to have a hand in shedding Royal blood, the party, or side, which should kill, or wound, him would expose themselves to great and irreparable mischiefs, in regard of the obligation that the whole Kingdom of the wounded, or slain, King hath to revenge him with the greatest destruction of their enemies, even with the certain loss of their own lives if it be needful. By how much such Kings are of greater dignity among them so much longer this obligation of furious revenge endureth. So that if the Samori should be killed, or wounded, by the Army of the King of Cocin, who is his enemy, but of greater dignity, the people of the Samori stand obliged to one day of revenge, (others say three days) during which everyone is obliged to act his utmost to the utter destruction of those of Cocin, even with the manifest hazard of his own life. But if the King of Cocin, who hath a greater repute, for honour at least, if not for power, should happen to be slain, or wounded, by the people of the Samori, the fury of revenge is to last in those of Cocin all the time of their lives (others say once a year), which would cause a great destruction of both sides. They call this term of time, or manner of revenge, _Amoco_; so that they say the _Amoco_ of the Samori lasts one day; the

Amoco of the King of Cocin lasts all the life, and so of others.[12]

This passage is interesting in its assertion that in at least some areas there existed a collective responsibility of the subjects of a king or lesser royal figure to avenge in a drastic manner any injury inflicted by another people on the leader or authority figure. The indication of differential periods of obligatory amoco determined by stature of the injured party is mentioned in no other source consulted in this investigation and would seem to be questionable, especially differentials of the magnitude described here. However, if this part of the account is accurate or partially accurate, it would lend support to the idea that the amok-like behavior involved was subject to control and regulation. It could be turned on and off and, in the areas of which Valle writes, would not have carried the inevitability of death for its practitioners.

Like Couto earlier, John Nieuhoff writes in 1662 of amok-like behavior and refers specifically to an amokos elite within the Nayar warriors caste. Particularly noteworthy here is the high honor accorded this group.

> Though the Nayros in general are very good soldiers, yet there is a certain kind among them called Amokos, who are esteemed above all the rest, being a company of stout, bold and desperate bravadoes. They oblige themselves by most direful imprecations against themselves and their families, calling heaven to witness, that they will revenge certain injuries done to their friends or patrons, which they certainly pursue with so much intrepidity, that they stop neither at fire nor sword, to take vengeance of the death of their master, but like mad men run upon the point of their enemies swords, which makes them be generally dreaded by all, and makes them to be in great esteem with their kings, who are accounted the more potent the greater number they entertain of those Amokos; tho' this their foolhardiness is chiefly attributed to the excessive use of the Amfion [opium]. You see the streets of all the towns on the Malabar coast full of

16

<u>Nayros</u> with their arms always about them, tho' many of them dwell in the country and a good number are kept near the king's person.[13]

Once again there is reference to a renowned martial elite, motivated to performance of amok-like acts. The element of preforay ritual is mentioned, Nieuhoff describing some of the substantive content of the ritualistic episode and supplementing the more formal components previously mentioned. But of primary importance here is, first, the assertion that significant esteem and honor accrued to the Amokos and therefore to those whom they served and, second, the indication that the acts of the Amokos may have taken place in the name of or on behalf of friends or patrons, and not only on behalf of kings and major authority figures.

That the Amokos were accorded special esteem is important in providing some possible sources of motivation for becoming one of their number. What rewards existed for such participation and behavior? First, it should be noted that Nayar warriors as a whole were shown great deference and occupied positions of considerable privilege. The accounts of Nieuhoff and Philip Baldaeus in the latter half of the seventeenth century agree that Nayars were considered nobility, in rank second only to Brahmans.[14] According to Nieuhoff:

> The Nayros . . . are descended of noble families, and brought up to the war. They appear with a shield on their left arm, which they carry aloft, and with a naked sword in the right hand. They are very haughty. . . . [They] were forced to give way to the Portuguese; but all other Malabars must give place to the Nayros. . . . Though the Nayros are from their infancy trained up to arms, and are very bold and brave, they are nevertheless very civil and meek in their conversation, according to the custom of that country; not withstanding which they are mightily addicted to robbing upon the highway, and will kill the travelers unawares. . . . This is the reason why the <u>Mahometan</u> Malabars dwelling in this country, whenever they are traveling from one place to another, take one of these Nayros along with

them, who is their conductor for a
certain piece of money, to the next
place where they take another, and by
this means may pass without any danger
. . . though their conductor should be
an old decrepit person, or only a
boy. . . . They will not converse with
any of the inferior orders . . .; nay,
if any of the vulgar sort happen only to
touch a Nayros as he passes by, he will
make his servant that carries his meat
after him, to throw it down upon the
ground; nay, if they do enter their
houses, or only touch the doors and
walls, they will not eat there for fear
of being defiled. However the Nayros
are not altogether so nice in these
points as the Brahmans. . . . Those
Nayros who are watching at the town
gates, and serve for conductors to
travelers, are the poorest of all [the
Nayars], yet will they rather follow
this employment than a trade, which they
look upon below their quality. They
apply themselves from their infancy to
the use of arms. . . . If a quarrel
happens to arise betwixt a Nayros and
another Malabar, the King allows the
latter a guard of another Nayros, and as
long as he stays with him, they dare not
fight . . . [To be included among the
Nayars] they must have the King's peculiar leave for it, and are afterwards
distinguished by a gold ring they wear
on the right arm, or by a [buffalo]
horn. . . . They would not have their
blood mixed with strangers or those of
inferior rank, of which they are so
cautious . . . for which reason, when
they walk abroad, they cry out aloud to
the common people, "popoire," keep back,
for if any of these should touch a
Nayros, he would certainly ruin him.[15]

It can be surmised that the amoucos or amokos,
an elite group amongst the Nayars, enjoyed a particularly high level of honor and prestige. They
were warriors among warriors, perhaps the most
esteemed among the esteemed, by oath dedicated to
die for a cause. Special recognition from the
public and one's peers, self-satisfaction, perhaps

special material benefits, a sense of fulfilling a divine mission to one's god, king or patron--these must have been the rewards motivating membership amongst the amokos and acceptance of a violent death when the time came. The final frenzied suicidal mission was the manner in which the members of this esteemed body met death. This was death with honor.

The reason for assigning importance to Nieuhoff's assertion that the amokos acted on behalf of friends and patrons as well as major authority figures lies in its implication that there may have been a gradual evolution from legitimized, honorable amok-like behavior within the martial collective on behalf of the injured or insulted leader to amok-like behavior on behalf of friend or patron (entrepreneurial amok) and finally, to solitary amok on behalf of oneself. While the early Indian accounts make practically no mention of this latter form of amok, a much later work makes it clear that solitary amok occurred with some frequency in the nineteenth century.[16] If this portrayal of the evolution of amok behavior in India is correct, it would seem reasonable to assume some carry-over of honor, respect, and awe to later more individualized manifestations. Thus, when organized martial amok in the manner thus far described became obsolete with the gradual adoption of firearms, residues of the cultural meanings originally adhering to the martial version remained.

A passage from Baldaeus's late seventeenth century work will serve as a final reference for India during this period. It is of special interest in that it refers to the Nayar elite collectively as amok--the spelling identical with that of the Malay term.

> Among the Nairos those who call themselves amok are the worst, being a company of desperadoes, who engage themselves and their families by oaths to revenge such injuries as are done them. They [Indonesian amok-runners, I assume] are often seen at Batavia. The power of the kings of Malabar is generally esteemed by the number of the Nairos under their jurisdiction. If any of their kings should be murdered, they would sacrifice all to revenge his death.[17]

19

Thus, Baldaeus likens the amok-runner of Batavia (present-day Jakarta) to the amok among the Nayars. As I have begun to demonstrate, a number of similarities indeed do exist between Indian and Malay varieties of amok--but there are also a number of significant differences.

Martial Amok in the Malay World

For greater Malaysia there are extant a somewhat limited number of references to amok prior to the nineteenth century. The references that do exist indicate an early presence of both martial and solitary amok, martial forms becoming less evident in the nineteenth century. Traced below are the historical outlines of the occurrence of amok in what is present-day Malaysia and Indonesia.

In Tome Pires' Suma Oriental is found the earliest reference to martial amok amongst Malays. It is included in a description of the conquest of Malacca in 1511 by the Portuguese under Alfons de Albuquerque. While the passage does not report the actual occurrence of amok, it does make clear that martial amok was a practice utilized by the Malays. According to Pires:

> The king never wanted peace, against the advice of his Lasamane and the Bemdara and his Cerina de Raja that he should make peace; but following his own counsel and that of his son, whom he afterwards killed, and of . . . other young nobles who offered to run completely amok for the king, he would hear nothing of peace. . . .[18]

Writing of the Portuguese conquest of Malacca, Sir Thomas Stamford Raffles records a translation of a Malayan history of the first arrival of the Portuguese at Malacca. The Portuguese ply the king with bounteous gifts and eventually ask for land on which they plan to build a military fortress.

> Alas! how often did the Bendahara and Tumungungs approach the Rajah with a request that the white men might not be permitted to build a large house: but the Rajah would say, "My eyes are upon them, and they are few in number: if they do any wrong, whatever it may be, I shall see it, and will give orders for

their being massacred, (literally, "I will order my men to amok, or as it is vulgarly termed, run a muck among them.")[19]

Eventually, the Portuguese easily took Malacca and completed their fortress, only to fall to a combined Malay and Dutch force.

> The men of Johore and the Dutch sailed for Malacca, and after attacking it for about fifteen days, from the sea, many were slain, as well Portuguese as Malays and Dutch. The Malays then held a consultation, and began to think, that if they fought against the white man according to this fashion, Malacca would not fall for ten years. It was therefore agreed upon by all the Malays, that fifty men should enter the fort of Malacca, and run a muck or meng-amok.
>
> The Malays then selected a lucky day, and on the twenty-first day of the month, at 5 o'clock in the morning, the fifty Malays entered the fort, and commenced amok, and every Portuguese was either put to death, or forced to fly into the interior of the country, without order or regularity.[20]

These two passages indicate that amok must have been a familiar military tactic in Malay regions by the sixteenth century. Whether or not the second passage is correct in detail does not matter so much as does the firm implication that amok existed as a military tactic and was thought to be of considerable utility.

A number of authors include references to the post-fifteenth century existence of martial amok in Malaysia and Indonesia. Perhaps the best documentation in this area is provided by Schrieke in a chapter on early Javanese warfare:

> The most feared of all Javanese military tactics was the surprise attack. The Dutch repeatedly fell victim to it, especially when they had overboldly ventured too far in battle. On such an occasion the cavalry attacked the enemy . . . "quite unexpectedly, like madmen,

21

with streaming hair, shaking their heads, with their lances in their hands." In such attacks, which were sometimes made at night, preference was given to falling upon the porters, in order to create confusion. Running amuck was a usual element in this kind of attack.[21]

Schrieke provides ample documentation for the existence of such practices and several of his citations bear repeating here. For instance, in 1624 during the siege of Madura by forces from the Javanese kingdom of Mataram:

> Two thousand Madurese in flight (turned back and) rushed like madmen among the army of Mataram, which was about fifty thousand men strong, . . . and ran amuck there, causing the (ruler of) Mataram a serious defeat, and seventeen of Mataram's highest officers, including the general of the army, as well as the tumenggung of Demak and other men of importance, besides some six thousand persons of lesser rank, were killed.[22]

Schrieke also cites the following case:

> The (ruler of) Mataram had sent twenty thousand men under the command of Tumenggung Alap-Alap ahead to Surabaja to destroy the crops and produce in the fields and to despoil the land, until he should despatch the main body of his army thither; . . . but the people of Surabaja, well taught by the success of the Madurese in running amuck, had also selected eight hundred of their men and sent them out before sunrise one morning to attack the troops of the (ruler of) Mataram; these, too, scored a triumph, killing many of the (Mataram) soldiers.[23]

Schrieke notes that throughout this period in Java the Dutch accounts make repeated reference to "amuck-runners." Again in 1680, he notes these tactics were used by Panembahan Mas of Giri when:

the army of the _susuhunan_, together with
some of the Dutch Company's troops, came
to force him to yield obedience to
Mangkurat II. When the troops appeared,
the aged saint urged his men "to such
violent defence and offence . . . as had
never been seen before in the east in
the course of this Javanese war."

They did not bother with shooting or
wounding in the struggle but, at the
constant cry _amokan_ (stab them to death)
of the aged _panembahan_, who personally
gave out his commands on every side,
they fell upon our men from all sides at
once, with such violence that after the
loss of six Europeans and ten Javanese
as well as a number of wounded, the
Madurese and Javanese of the _susuhunan_
fell into so much confusion that they
grew panicky and took flight, thereby at
the same time completely disorganizing
two of our white companies and putting a
third to flight.[24]

A final citation from the work of Schrieke is
of interest in its demonstration that the amok
tactic was also utilized for purposes of more
limited massacre and not solely in large-scale
battles. A well-known event of seventeenth century
Java, the attack on the ambassador and commissioner
Francois Tak at Kartasura in 1686, saw the tactic
employed in this fashion. When Tak arrived

such was the confusion at the Javanese
court and among the disgruntled Balinese
rogues residing there . . . that a surprise attack was made on Commissioner
Tak and his suite by Amuck-runners,
either by these Balinese on their own
account or with the approval of the
Javanese nobles; as a result . . . Tak
after long resistance perished in
anguish from his many wounds before the
susuhunan's court, as also (five other
Dutch officials and military figures)
. . . together with sixty-nine (other)
whites.[25]

In his classic _History of Java_, Raffles in
1817 depicts martial amok thusly:

The phrenzy generally known by the term
muck or amok, is only another form of
that fit of desperation which bears the
same name among the military, and under
the influence of which they rush upon
the enemy, or attack a battery, in the
manner of a forlorn hope. The accounts
of the wars of the Javans, as well as of
the Malayus, abound with instances of
warriors running amok; of combatants,
giving up all idea of preserving their
own lives, rushing on the enemy, committing indiscriminate slaughter, and never
surrendering themselves alive.[26]

Another passage from Raffles' work is especially interesting in its indication that amok was
sometimes an almost automatic individual and
collective response to a felt affront to one's
dignity and to the dignity of one's leader. The
year is 1717.

Pangeran Chakra Deningrat . . . resolved
to throw himself on the protection of
the Dutch . . . the admiral instructed
the captain (of a Dutch ship) to take
the chief and his family on board, and
convey them to (Surabaya). The captain
immediately sent a messenger on shore to
the Pangeran, informing him of the
wishes of the admiral, and inviting him
to come on board with his family.
Pangeran Chakra Deningrat, who was
unconscious of treachery or duplicity,
and consequently void of suspicion,
. . . accepted the invitation, and,
accompanied by his family, immediately
went off in a small fishing boat. When
arrived alongside of the ship, the
followers who carried the upachara
(emblems of state) were ordered to go on
board: after them the Pangeran himself
ascended, and then his wife, Raden Ayu
Chakra Deningrat. When the Pangeran
came upon deck, Captain Curtis took him
by the hand, and delivered him over to
one of his officers, who immediately led
him into the cabin. The captain
remained till the Raden Ayu had
ascended, and as soon as she came on
deck he likewise took her by the hand,

and after the European manner kissed her cheek. Not understanding the custom she became alarmed, and thinking that Captain Curtis was offering an insult to her, screamed out, and called aloud upon her husband, saying the "Captain had evil intentions." The _Pangeran_ hearing the cries of his wife became furious, and drawing his _kris_ rushed out, and without further inquiry stabbed the Captain. The attendants of the chief, who had come on board with the state ornaments, following the example of their master, raised the cry of _amok_ and immediately fell on the crew of the vessel. The latter, however, were too powerful for them, and in a short time the whole of the Madurese party were killed, together with the chief and his wife.[27]

In Crawfurd's important historical work of 1820, _History of the Indian Archipelago_, we find the following:

The Indian Islanders apply the word muck to the charge of Europeans with the bayonet, but this arises from their associating it with the partial charges made now and then in their own mode of warfare, by a few devoted and insulated individuals, and which are real acts of desperation, in which the calculation of success is quite overbalanced by that of failure.[28]

Gullick reports the prominent use of the tactic of surprise attack and provides additional reasons for its use in nineteenth century Malaya. Gullick states that most Malayan warfare at this time consisted of very limited conflicts between two chiefs and their respective followers. Most fighting was a "desultory affair of raids" with wars generally fought "as a means of 'self-help' to obtain revenge and also to adjust the balance of power within the State."[29] Occasionally, there occurred opposing coalitions of warring chiefs.[30] In nearly all instances operations were short-run. The surprise attack with its amok-runners was particularly well-suited to this manner of warfare. According to Gullick:

The typical operation began with the departure of a raiding party which endeavored to approach the enemy stockade unobserved so as to capture it by a single desperate rush before the defenders could rally. If these tactics failed or could not be employed, the attackers either withdrew or tried to take the stockade without severe fighting. . . . Determined attacks on prepared positions, with the inevitable consequence of heavy casualties, were not favored. Victory at the price of a long list of killed or wounded would soon demoralize the followers of any leader who resorted to such tactics.[31]

It was not just tactical utility but tradition and custom as well that accounted for the Malays' continued use of marital amok far into the nineteenth century. The Javanese, Raffles asserts, "in their tactics and conduct . . . endeavor to emulate the examples given in their ancient romances; and in the plan for their pitched battles, the march of their armies, and the individual heroism of their chiefs, they strive to imitate the romantic exhibitions in the poems of antiquity."[32] Raffles' work includes translations of various Javanese ethical codes which include references to the merits of surprise attacks. One such code, referred to by Raffles as the Niti sastra, includes the following passage:

A chief should keep his plan of attack as secret as possible, because the knowledge of it may enable the enemy to be on guard, and turn the measures taken to his own advantage. He ought not to challenge his enemy to give battle, as in that case the enemy will have an opportunity of preparing himself for the same: but he should attempt to surprise him, and rush upon him like a fire, that quickly and without much noise consumeth all with which it comes in contact.[33]

The Niti sastra also informs us that the man who falls in such an engagement can expect heavenly rewards: "the warrior killed in battle, who is like a conqueror, (will) enjoy all the delight imaginable."[34]

26

Referring more specifically to employment of amok behavior in battle, Alfred Wallace states as follows:

> In their wars a whole regiment of these people will sometimes agree to "amok," and then rush on with such energetic desperation as to be very formidable to men not so excited as themselves. Among the ancients these would have been looked upon as heroes or demigods who sacrificed themselves for their country."[35]

Likewise, Galloway notes the historical existence of martial amok and indicates the importance of tradition in its occurrence. Galloway writes the following:

> The term "amok" means quite as much the act of a number of persons as of an individual, and was the term used to describe the tribal raids which were so common in the various states of [Malaya] . . . in the early and middle parts of [the nineteenth century] and still are . . . in some parts of Central Borneo.
>
> In these raids . . ., the aggressors [were] . . . in a "mad humour of killing," the defenders, knowing there was no mercy to be expected, fought to a finish. . . . these raids were not, as a rule, undertaken for plunder. They were usually the outcome of the public recital, continued for days or weeks, of some time-honoured hero's exploits and accomplishments, until each hand clutched kris or parang in a nervy grasp and each felt himself seized by the bloodthirst. . . . The term as indicating collective action is now obsolete, although Marsden says that it is still applied in relation to animals.[36]

Summary and Comparison:
Indian and Malay Martial Amok

Over the sixteenth and seventeenth centuries in southern India there appears to have occurred a gradual evolution from obligatory amok-like acts

27

performed by an esteemed on-going martial contingent, occasionally joined by other warriors motivated by a sudden dramatic setback in battle, toward a rather more "decentralized" amok, wherein a person engages in or poses the threat of amok-like acts as a service-for-hire. There is virtually no evidence during this period of the occurrence of individualized, solitary amok although solitary amok does occur in nineteenth century India, by which time martial amok and amok as a service for hire apparently had nearly or fully disappeared. Besides its institutionalized nature, amok-like behavior in southern India included a degree of discrimination in selection of victims--a feature to some extent differentiating it from the more randomly-directed solitary amok of the nineteenth century Malay world. The sources of motivation for the more calculated, premeditated amok of the on-going martial contingents of sixteenth and seventeenth century India appear to have included social honor and prestige, a high degree of deference from peers and the public, and perhaps material benefits and concessions. As amok-like behavior decreased in utility as a military tactic, its civilian manifestations were accorded residually some of the honor and legitimacy originally adhering to martial amok.

Among Malays, it has been demonstrated that martial amok was a prominent practice dating at least from the period of first significant European contact until well into the nineteenth century. As in India, martial amok was viewed as honorable behavior. At some dim point in history, the practice itself may have originated in one of these two areas with subsequent transmission to the other area. Regardless of the exact nature of the relationship between India and Malay areas it is the culturally-defined honor adhering to martial amok that is important in explaining the partial legitimacy that Malays accorded to solitary amok.

A further similarity with India is that in Malay martial amok the choice of victims was not totally indiscriminate and random. Military-based amok-runners apparently aimed their efforts only at opponents. Completely random killing would have meant a loss of utility for amok as a martial tactic since friend and foe alike would have fallen victim to the amok-runner.

Several differences are also evident between Indian and Malayan martial amok. First, available evidence in the Malayan context does not indicate the existence of on-going organized martial contingents specializing in martial amok. Rather, for Malays, martial amok appears to have been a less formalized, but nevertheless understood behavioral expectation of the warrior. Probably an important reason for the apparently more informal nature of Malay martial amok was the limited nature of much Malay warfare, which often consisted of simple raiding engagements between two chiefs with small bands of followers. A second important difference between the Indian and Malayan cases is that there are for the Malay regions repeated references to instances of solitary, individualized amok occurring contemporaneously with martial amok. For as far back as the record takes us, solitary amok appears to have been a prominent event in Malay life and, in the end, the solitary version outlasted the martial.

Chapter 3

SOLITARY AMOK IN THE MALAY WORLD:
A CHRONOLOGY AND SELECTED CASES

We now present a chronological review of
references to amok behavior engaged in by lone
individuals outside the military context. The
descriptions of six episodes which are presented
collectively illustrate both the range of behaviors
associated with solitary amok and the reactions of
others to amok-runners.

<u>Solitary Amok: A Chronology</u>

The earliest recorded reference to solitary
amok found in this investigation comes from Nicolo
Conti writing in the early fifteenth century,
although he did not use the word itself. With the
geographic referent either Java or Sumbawa, Conti
states:

> They regard killing as a mere jest, nor
> is any punishment allotted for such a
> deed. Debtors are given up to their
> creditors to be their slaves. But he
> who, rather than be a slave, prefers
> death, seizing a naked sword issues into
> the street and kills all he meets, until
> he is slain by some one more powerful
> than himself: then comes the creditor of
> the dead man and cites him by whom he
> was killed, demanding of him his debt,
> which he is constrained by the judges to
> satisfy.[1]

Thus, at this very early date Conti depicts
the solitary amok-runner (<u>pengamok</u>) incited to
indiscriminate mass murder by the operation of a
social system that forces him almost irrevocably
into slavery and social disrepute. This attribution
of etiology to the nature of social relationships is
occasionally repeated and enlarged upon in the

attempts made in the ensuing five centuries to account for the occurrence of amok. The matter shall be given further consideration in later chapters.

The next recorded reference to solitary amok appears in 1516 in the journals of the Portuguese Duarte Barbosa. The geographic referent is Java. The passage permits the inference that amok was a rather well-established and familiar practice by the sixteenth century.

> There are some of them (Javanese) who if they fall ill of any severe illness vow to God that if they remain in health they will of their own accord seek another more honourable death for his service, and as soon as they get well they take a dagger in their hands, and go out into the streets and kill as many persons as they meet, both men, women, and children, in such wise that they go like mad dogs, killing until they are killed. These are called <u>amuco</u>. And as soon as they see them begin this work, they cry out, saying <u>amuco</u>, <u>amuco</u>, in order that people may take care of themselves, and they kill them with dagger and spear thrusts.[2]

The assertion that amok is a religiously-motivated response upon recovery from severe illness is not repeated elsewhere in the literature although, as we will see, several early twentieth century authors attribute amok to individuals concurrently experiencing malarial or other tropical fever delirium states. But the passage is more noteworthy in several other respects. The assignment of at least quasi-religious motivation to the act points up a component sometimes present in descriptions and explanations of amok and amok-like acts, particularly outside the borders of present-day Malaysia and Indonesia. Also, the spear and dagger weaponry, the indiscriminate murderous foray, the warning cry and the death-dealing response of the community--are all features often present in the episodes of solitary amok that form the major focus of this investigation.

While the majority of references to solitary amok do not appear until the late eighteenth and nineteenth centuries, the comments of several authors prior to this time should be cited so as to demonstrate that the pattern did not disappear temporarily during the seventeenth and eighteenth centuries. Chapter two included the 1602 reference by Couto to solitary amok among the Javanese. The journals of the 1604-1606 voyage of Sir Henry Middleton to the Moluccas report, "If any Javan have committed a fact worthy of death and that he be pursued by any, whereby he thinketh hee shall die, he will presently draw his weapon and cry Amucke . . .; not sparing to murther either man, woman, or childe which they can possibly come at; and he that killeth most dieth with greatest honor and credit."[3] In 1659, a Dutchman, Wouter Schouten, relates that

> I saw in this month of February at Batavia the breasts torn with red-hot tongs off a black Indian by the executioner; and after this he was broken on the wheel from below upwards. This was because through the evil habit of eating opium . . . he had become mad and raised the cry of Amocle . . . in which mad state he had slain five persons. . . . This was the third Amocle-cryer whom I saw during that visit to Batavia (a few months) broken on the wheel for murder. . . .
>
> Such a murderer and Amocle-runner has sometimes the fame of being an invincible hero because he has so manfully repulsed all who tried to seize him. . . . So the Netherlands Government is compelled when such an Amocle-runner is taken alive to punish him in a terrific manner.[4]

Especially interesting in these passages from the Middleton journals and Schouten is the assignment of honor and merit to the amok-runner. Neither passage asserts that the assignment of honor inevitably accompanies solitary amok, but they do make clear that this was a possible outcome. And it is this possibility that aids us in understanding the historic quasi-legitimacy accorded amok. That the amok-runner is sometimes viewed as an "invincible hero" is indicative of a positive correlation between the honor accorded him and the desirability of and need for such behavior in the martial context. It is also a reflection of the merit attached to such behavior in the ancient tales and ethical codes praising and encouraging individual prowess.

The Dutch East India Company Records relate that in 1720 the leader of the Buginese at Tanjong Kling in Perak ran amok when his leader, one Daeng Marewa, confronted him with the accusation that he had spread malicious rumors concerning Daeng Marewa's activities.[5] At this point another fifty-year gap occurs in the recorded instances of amok. Then, during the period of 1768-1771, the Dutch voyager, Johan Stavorinus, visits Batavia and describes, if not very accurately, the occurrence of amok. Amok is attributed largely to excessive consumption of opium and is said to be primarily the act of slaves coming from the Celebes, especially the Buginese.[6] According to Stavorinus:

> These acts of indiscriminate murder, are called by us <u>mucks</u>. . . . When . . . raised to a pitch of desperate fury, they sally out with a knife, or other weapon, in their hand, and kill, without distinction of sex, rank, or age, whoever they meet in the streets of Batavia; and proceed in this way, till they are either shot dead, or taken prisoner. . . . They run in upon the arms opposed to them, and often kill their opponents, even after they are themselves mortally wounded. . . . Many instances of <u>mucks</u> occurred, during my residence at <u>Batavia</u>; they were mostly done in the evening.[7]

An especially interesting case of solitary amok is reported in Perak in 1777. The case is unusual in that the perpetrator is of royal stature and because there exist both Dutch and Malay accounts of the same episode. According to the Dutch account, on March 15, 1777, a son of the Raja Bendahara, married to a daughter of the Raja Muda (his cousin), fell into a rage and took the life of his wife, his own child, the sister of his wife (married to another prince), together with two children and six slaves.[8] He then set fire to his house, with several other houses catching fire and burning as a result. A son of the Raja Muda, about twelve years old, escaped and with his mother and three other men who were attempting to flee to the "reigning king." By <u>prahu</u> the amok prince set after

34

and overtook them. The mother of the young prince sprang into the water and escaped into the jungle. A Malay who tried to rescue the young prince was repeatedly stabbed. The young prince managed to escape unwounded. The amok-runner then sailed to the home of the king and, at about eight o'clock, met up with two Chinese, killing one while the other fled. He then went to the king's residence and opened the door. There he was confronted by his father, the Raja Bendahara, who pushed him away and knocked a kris from his hand. Attempting to punish his son, the Raja Bendahara put his foot on the kris. However, the son wrested it free and stabbed his father. The king then stabbed the prince with a kris, and he fell to the earth. He then arose and attempted to flee. Six men were needed to overcome the badly wounded amok prince. "Whereupon he fell to earth and passed away."

According to the Malay version of the same episode, Raja 'Abdu'r-Rahim lost his akal (mind, intellect) because he saw his child's nurse angry with her charge.[9] This loss of composure by a royal personage is strictly forbidden in Malay royal custom, according to the text. He slapped the nurse, who repeatedly parried the blow with the child whom she was carrying on her hip. Seeing that his own child was being struck, 'Abdu'r-Rahim drew his kris. Again the child was used to parry the blow, and when he saw that his son was wounded, the Raja killed the nurse, and also stabbed his wife as she came up from her bathing place. He burnt his house, and tried to run amok in the palace, but was killed by his father, Raja Bendahara. From there- after the name 'Abdu'r-Rahim became tabu to Perak Rajas.

The assertion in the Malay manuscript that the name of 'Abdu'r-Rahim thereafter became tabu may indicate that this version was recorded after a sub- stantial passage of time following the actual event. If so, one might assume greater accuracy in the apparently contemporaneous Dutch account. However, it is the congruences and not the discrepancies in the two versions that are of importance. Both accounts very definitely report that the perpetrator was of royal status. Though such cases appear to be rare, the practice of amok was not limited to mem- bers of relatively deprived social strata. To the extent that royal personages and other individuals of social stature did commit solitary amok, this might be counted, if tenuously, as another source of legitimacy for similar engagement by individuals of lesser social stature.

With the approach of the nineteenth century and the increased presence of the British, there occurs an increase in the frequency of reports of solitary amok. This is apparently due to the fact that there were suddenly many more individuals present who recorded such events in English; in fact, who recorded them at all. The British colonial period and the period immediately prior to it serves as the temporal frame for the large majority of recorded cases of solitary amok. Much of the remainder of this analysis will center on these cases, utilizing them to assess the explanations tendered for their occurrence, and as a base on which to formulate revised explanatory statements.

In 1784, William Marsden in his History of Sumatra writes: "It is not to be controverted, that those desperate acts of indiscriminate murder, called by us, mucks, and by the natives, mengamok, do actually take place, and frequently too, in some parts of the East (in Java in particular). . . ."[10] However, Marsden goes on to indicate that amok was a very infrequent event during his residency at Bencoolen on the west coast of Sumatra. He reports being eyewitness to only one case of amok during this period, and the case he describes bears few of the characteristics of mengamok.

Crawfurd describes briefly two cases of amok occurring in 1812. First:

> The Bugis slave of a Creole Dutch woman at Surabaya in Java ran a muck. . . . His wife, who had been more particularly the object of the cruelty of the mistress, he first put to death, and after her his three children. With the youngest infant he rushed out into the street, holding the bloody axe with which he had perpetrated the first murders in his hand, and, in the presence of two English gentlemen, decapitated the infant, on which he threw the weapon from him into the neighboring canal, and surrendered himself to the gentlemen, begging them to take his life.[11]

And second:

In the year 1812, the very day on which the fortified palace of the sultan of Java was stormed, a certain petty chief, a favourite of the dethroned sultan, was one of the first to come over to the conquerors, and was active, in the course of the day, in carrying into effect the successful measures pursued for the pacification of the country. At night he was, with many other Javanese, hospitably received into the spacious house of the chief of the Chinese, and appeared to be perfectly satisfied with the new order of things. The house was protected by a strong guard of Sepoys. At night, without any warning, but, starting from his sleep, he commenced havock, and, before he had lost his own life, killed and wounded a great number of persons, chiefly his countrymen, who were sleeping in the same apartment with him.[12]

Respectively, these two cases include two noteworthy elements. In the first, the amok-runner commits homicidal acts against his closest relatives. In this case, the episode is wholly constituted of such acts; a more common pattern finds kin-directed homicide initiating the episode, followed by fully indiscriminate homicide. In either case, the attacks on blood relatives suggest other than total randomness in victim selection. Unless this is merely a function of propinquity, an element of selectivity appears present, suggesting a degree of intellectual control and intentionality.

The second case also includes a feature common to many amok episodes: the acts are committed against and in the presence of a totally unsuspecting group of victims and observers. There was no prior warning and no precipitating cause (unless the pengamok was purposely avenging the sultan). Many cases of amok are marked by a spontaneous, motiveless quality. Even in cases where the amok-runner had been observed to engage in a period of brooding and unease prior to running amok, the survivors of the attack who had observed this never indicated that they anticipated that amok would ensue.

In an 1823 Singapore episode identified as amok, premeditation and a degree of restrained calculation is evident. The case received substantial contemporary and historic notoriety probably because a prominent British Resident was attacked and wounded in the fray. The official treatment accorded the offender following the attack is also of special interest.

On the 11th March, Colonel Farquhar was severely stabbed by an Arab named Syed Yassin, who ran amok. On that morning, Syed Omar . . . had sued Syed Yassin for the value of some goods he had sold to him. . . . Colonel Farquhar gave judgment for Syed Omar for $1,400, and Syed Yassin said he had not the money to pay. Syed Omar replied that he had the money, but would not pay, and Colonel Farquhar said that he must either pay, or give proper security, or go to jail, for imprisonment for debt was . . . then in force.

The imprisonment of a Syed (or Holy man) was an insult to a descendant of the Prophet . . . and he planned his revenge . . . in an artful way. He was taken to the jail . . . ; but he had hidden his kris inside his coat. About five o'clock he asked . . . the Magistrate to allow him to see Syed Omar, and try to prevail on him to give him time to pay. [The Magistrate] allowed it, and sent a Hindoo peon in charge of him. . . .

Syed Yassin entered the compound of Syed Omar's house to kill him. The peon stopped at the outer gate, and when Syed Omar saw Syed Yassin coming in, he guessed his intention from his countenance, and ran out the back door . . . to Colonel Farquhar's house . . . and told him that Syed Yassin had rushed at him at his house with a drawn kris. Colonel Farquhar . . . went out to Syed Omar's house. In the meantime, the peon finding that Syed Yassin did not come out, called to him to come away . . . and Syed Yassin went to the gate and stabbed the peon, who fell down dead at his feet.

Colonel Farquhar [and at least eight other individuals] all went into the compound [of Syed Omar's house], in the centre of which . . . was the usual square place, where natives used to sit and talk, called the balei. . . . The murderer when he saw them approaching, had hidden under the balei. . . .

[Colonel Farquhar] went up to the balei and pushed about with his stick underneath it, when Syed Yassin suddenly made a crouching spring at him and stabbed him in the chest. . . . Abdulla [Munshi] and Andrew Farquhar ran up and supported him, and the latter having a sword in his hand cut Syed Yassin's mouth right through to his ear, and the Sepoys seeing this thrust him through with their bayonets. . . .

A crowd of Europeans and Natives . . . assembled around Syed Omar's house. Sir Stamford Raffles came in his carriage, and in great haste ran into the Colonel's house, and finding that he was not killed . . . took up a candle and went to see the body of Syed Yassin.

Just at this time, a person going with a torch into Syed Omar's compound, stumbled over the dead body of the Hindoo peon, and then a fresh hubbub arose. Sir Stamford . . . asked who Syed Yassin was, but his body by this time was so cut about by the infuriated people that it could not be recognized. . . . When the crowd had cleared away . . . four . . . convicts came and tied a rope to Syed Yassin's feet, and dragged the corpse to the centre of the plain. Raffles then ordered a blacksmith to be called, and when he came with three others, he scored on the sand a thing in the shape of a box, to be made of iron bars like a cage, about the height of a man, and said it must be made that night. . . .

The next morning Sir Stamford went to the Colonel's house, and the Sultan and Tumongong and their chiefs came, and all the Europeans. The natives were called, and it was decided that the corpse should be sent around the town, in a buffalo cart, and the gong beaten to tell the people what he had done; and after that hung up in an iron cage . . . on a mast . . . [to remain] there for a fortnight. On the 14th March, Raffles published a proclamation stating that the Sultan in the name of the Malays had requested pardon of the King of England and the body was allowed to be removed, but all must take notice that amokers would be hung in chains and their bodies given to the winds. . . .

This was the first amok we have any record of here [Singapore]. They are now [1902] rare, although in former times, and not very long ago, they were frequent enough.[13]

The severity of the posthumous treatment of Syed Yassin appears not to have generated contemporary or historic moralistic indignation, as opposed to the actions of Sir William Norris in 1846 in the infamous case of Sunan, to be reviewed shortly. Remembering the context aids one in understanding Raffles' action. First, as indicated in the passages cited earlier from his History of Java, Raffles was intimately familiar with the practice of amok from his earlier experiences in Malaya and Java. He probably knew and understood amok as well as any other non-Malay. More important, however, the settlement of Singapore was but four years old at the time of Syed Yassin's amok, with a very small number of Europeans in the midst of a native community of perhaps ten thousand persons. British preeminence in Singapore was not as yet comfortably established, and Raffles' actions were undoubtedly designed to convey dramatically to an impressionable native community the fact of British dominance.

Solitary Amok: Selected Cases

For the period of 1825 to 1925, the sources consulted in this study include references to and descriptions of approximately fifty separate episodes of solitary amok. These vary in extent from one or two-sentence news accounts to chapter-long descriptions and analyses. The many accounts reveal such a multiplicity of variations on the solitary amok theme that it becomes impossible to select several particular episodes and present them as fully representative of the universe. Consequently, what follows are six episodes, selected not because they necessarily represent "typical" cases of nineteenth and early twentieth century solitary amok, but because the six cases in their totality appear to include most of the relevant dimensions included in the universe of solitary amok among Malays during the 1825-1925 period. While the review of materials relating to post-1925 Malaysia and Indonesia had been considerably less thorough than for the preceding years, it appears that full-scale episodes of solitary amok became very rare, particularly in those areas most penetrated by modern influences. Thus, it is primarily amok-related phenomena of the nineteenth and early twentieth centuries to which attention must be directed, and these six cases, along with that of Imam Mamat reported earlier, provide an important set of data from which to launch a more intensive analysis of solitary amok. The cases are presented with only brief comments specifying the highlights of each episode.

Case 1: Sunan

What follows is an account of the judicial disposition of one case of amok in Penang. The judicial statement is preceded by a descriptive passage written by J. R. Logan, the editor of the journal in which the statement was printed. According to Logan:

> On the 8th July 1846, Sunan, a respectable Malay house-builder in Pinang, ran amok . . ., and before he was arrested killed an old Hindu woman, a Kling, a Chinese boy, and a Kling girl about 3 years old in the arms of its father, and wounded two Hindus, three Klings, and two Chinese, of whom only two survived. On his trial it appeared that he was greatly afflicted by the recent loss of his wife and child, which preyed upon his mind and quite altered his appearance. A person with whom he had lived up to the 15th of June said further "He used to bring his child to his work,

41

since its death he has worked for me; he often said he could not work as he was affected by the loss of his child. I think he was out of his mind, he did not smoke or drink, I think he was mad." On the morning of the amok this person met him, and asked him to work at his boat. "He replied that he could not, he was very much afflicted." "He had his hands concealed under his cloth, he frequently exclaimed, Allah, Allah!" "He daily complained of the loss of his wife and child." On the trial Sunan declared he did not know what he was about, and persisted in this at the place of execution, adding "As the gentlemen say I have committed so many murders I suppose it must be so." The amok took place on the 8th, the trial on the 13th, and the execution on the 15th July--all within eight days."[14]

Particularly noteworthy in this case is the indication that Sunan had experienced prolonged grief over the death of his wife and child. As suggested in Logan's comment and in the judge's remarks presented below, amok may have been a willful, vengeful response to the overwhelming psychological blow with which Sunan had been visited. In his despair, he would show the capricious fates, as well as his fellow man, that he was a force with which to be reckoned. He would end his now empty life in heroic style; he would run amok.

The swift disposition of Sunan's case was carried out in the court of the Recorder of Penang, Sir William Norris. The judge's statement is an interesting example of God-fearing colonial self-righteousness and judicial overkill. In conferring a sentence of death and finding Sunan's Islamic faith to be the basic causal factor, the judge made these remarks:

Sunan, you stand convicted on the clearest evidence of the wilful murder of Pakir Sah on Wednesday last and it appears that on the same occasion you stabbed no less than 10 other unfortunate persons, only 2 of whom are at present surviving. It now becomes my duty to pass upon you the last sentence of the law. I can scarcely call it a

42

painful duty, for the blood of your innocent victims cries aloud for vengeance and both justice and humanity would be shocked were you permitted to escape the infamy of a public execution. God Almighty alone, the great "searcher of hearts," can tell precisely what passed in that wretched heart of your's before and at the time when you committed these atrocious deeds; nor is it necessary for the ends of justice that we should perfectly comprehend the morbid views and turbulent passions by which you must have been actuated. It is enough for us to know that you, like all other murderers, "had not the fear of God before your eyes," and that you acted "of malice aforethought and by the instigation of the devil" himself, who was "a murderer from the beginning." But all the atrocities you have committed are of a peculiar character and such as are never perpetrated by Christians, Hindoos, Chinese, or any other class than Mahomedans, especially Malays, among whom they are frightfully common, and may therefore be justly branded by way of infamous distinction, as Mahomedan Murders. I think it right, therefore, seeing so great a concourse of Mahomedans in and about the Court, to take this opportunity of endeavouring to disabuse their minds and your own of any false notions of courage, heroism, or self devotion which Mahomedans possibly, but Mahomedans alone of all mankind, can ever attach to such base, cowardly and brutal murders; notions which none but the devil himself, "the father of lies," could ever have inspired. But if such false, execrable and dangerous delusions really are entertained by any man or body of men whatever, it may be as well to show from the gloomy workings of your mind, so far as circumstances have revealed them, that not a particle of manly courage or heroism could have animated you, or can ever animate any man who lifts his cowardly hand against helpless women and children. You had deaths of your wife and only child, and

43

God forbid that I should needlessly
harrow up your feelings by reverting to
the subject. I do so merely because it
serves in some degree to explain the
dreadful tragedy for which you are now
about to answer with your life. Unable
or unwilling to submit with patience to
the affliction with which it had pleased
God to visit you, you abandoned yourself
to discontent and despair, until shortly
before the bloody transaction, when you
went to the mosque to pray!!--to pray to
whom or to what? Not to senseless Idols
of wood or stone which Christians and
Mahomedans equally abominate--but to the
one omniscient, almighty, and all merciful God in whom alone Christians and
Mahomedans profess to believe! But in
what spirit did you pray, if you prayed
at all? Did you pray for resignation or
ability to "humble yourself under the
mighty hand of God?" Impossible. You
may have gone to curse in your heart and
gnash with your teeth, but certainly not
to pray, whatever unmeaning sentences of
the Koran may have issued from your
lips. Doubtless you entered the Mosque
with a heart full of haughty pride,
anger and rebellion against your maker,
and no wonder that, when thus abandoned
to the devil, you stabbed with equal
cruelty, cowardice and ferocity unarmed
and helpless men, women and children,
who had never injured, never known,
probably never seen you before.

Such are the murders which
Mahomedans alone have been found capable
of committing. Not that I mean to brand
Mahomedans in general as worse than all
other men, far from it; I believe there
are many good men among them,--as good
as men can be who are ignorant of the
only true religion. I merely state the
fact that such atrocities disgrace no
other creed, let the Mahomedans account
for the fact as they may. But whatever
may be the true explanation; whether
these fiendish excesses are the result
of fanaticism, superstition, overweening
pride or ungovernable rage, or, which is

44

probable, of all combined, public justice demands that the perpetrators should be visited with the severest and most disgraceful punishment which the law can inflict.

The sentence of the Court therefore is, that you, Sunan, be remanded to the place from whence you came, and that on the morning of Wednesday next you be drawn from thence on a hurdle to the place of execution, and there hanged by the neck until you are dead. Your body will then be handed over to the surgeons for dissection, and your mangled limbs, instead of being restored to your friends for decent interment, will be cast into the sea, thrown into a ditch, or scattered on the earth at the discretion of the Sheriff. And may God Almighty have mercy on your miserable soul![15]

Case 2: Hadji Ibrahim

This account, written by W. Gilmore Ellis, who at the time was Medical Superintendent of the Government Asylum in Singapore, describes a rather common pattern. A sea-faring Malay, often Buginese, temporarily resident in one of the port cities of the Peninsula, suddenly and seemingly inexplicably runs amok. As with Hadji Ibrahim, the actions frequently appear wholly spontaneous and motiveless. Generally, most of his victims are unknown to him, just as he and his background are virtually unknown to anyone in the urban setting. With so little known about the amok-runner, attempts to assess etiology were highly speculative. Even in cases like that of Hadji Ibrahim where a capture was effected and the amok-runner found insane and incarcerated in an asylum, subsequent inquiry generally led to very little in the way of definitive explanations.

On November 5th, 1887 [in Singapore], there were sleeping in one room Mamoot (a boy, about 16), Ahamat (the owner of the house), a Malay girl, Hadji Ibrahim (a Bugis trader), and his brother Aboo. At about 11:30 p.m., Hadji Ibrahim suddenly got up and attacked Ahamat with

45

a long cutting and pointed knife,
inflicting an incised wound down to the
bone of the left temple, a long deep
incised wound on the left shoulder, a
deep incised wound in the middle of the
back, an incised wound of the front of
the left side of the thorax, penetrating
through the ribs to the lung, a stab on
the left side of the abdomen, wounding
the intestines, and there were deep
gashes on the hands and forearms. During this attack Mamoot, Aboo, and the
girl ran away into the street; they were
all asleep when the attack commenced.
Hadji Ibrahim must now have jumped out
of a window into the back court of an
adjoining house, which he found open.
He entered this house, and went upstairs
into a room, where he found Mariam and
Umborasih (two Malay women) sewing, and
a man named Syed asleep. He immediately
rushed across the room and stabbed
Mariam several times in the back, and
Syed in five places. Mariam and
Umborasih ran downstairs, and Hadji
Ibrahim left Syed and followed them,
stabbing Mariam again and Umborasih to
the heart. None of Mariam's wounds were
very serious, but Syed had several
severe cuts and stabs. Continuing the
Amok, Hadji Ibrahim ran out of the house
into the street, meeting Mariam's husband at the door; making two ineffectual
stabs at him as he passed, he ran on up
the street. Neither Mariam, Syed,
Umborasih, or Mariam's husband knew
Hadji Ibrahim. In the street the first
man he met was a Kling, and him he
stabbed in the chest and twice in the
right forearm. Further on he met two
Chinamen; one ran safely away, but the
other was stabbed in the abdomen, the
knife passing through liver, intestines,
and stomach. The next to be met was a
Malay named Bakar, whom he stabbed in
the forearm as he ran by to attack a
Malay named Sed. Sed grasped the knife
with his hands and a struggle ensued, in
which Hadji Ibrahim lost his weapon and
Sed obtained two slight wounds. The
Amoker now ran off unarmed, and was

chased, by Sed and other people who had come up, into the arms of a native constable, by whom he was arrested. Ahamat, Umborasih, and the Chinamen were picked up dead; the five wounded persons recovered. The prisoner, when arrested, had an excited, hunted expression, was sullen, and refused to answer questions bearing on his crime, but I can glean no further information as to his condition. At the assizes he was found too insane to plead. He first came under my notice rather more than a year after the crime, and there is little to be said about him. He was a tall, spare man, about 40 years old, pitted with small-pox marks, with a quick, irregular heart's action, and a wild stare in his eyes. He rarely spoke unless addressed, but was perfectly rational and coherent in his answers. He was cleanly and industrious, and slept and ate well. When spoken to about his Amok, he always became somewhat confused, and persisted in saying that he remembered absolutely nothing about it. At the present time he is fairly cheerful, quite rational and coherent, memory very fair, in good physical health, but his heart is slightly hypertrophied, pulse hard, and heart's action somewhat irregular. Although he knows that any confession can now make no difference to his future, he still denies any recollection of the Amok, and says, "As you state I committed these murders and murderous assaults, I suppose I did, but I remember nothing of it."[16]

Case 3: Ngah Gafur

In The Real Malay, Frank Swettenham included the following newspaper account of solitary amok. The setting is rural Perak in the 1890's. Marital and family stress offer a possible motive. Blood relatives are initially attacked, followed by random victims. The prolonged period of the episode and the continuing acts of aggression are similar to the case of Imam Mamat reported in Chapter one, suggesting that something more than temporary fever-induced delirium was moving the amok-runner. As opposed to an urban setting, a rural locale, with better opportunities to evade pursuers, might make possible a more prolonged amok episode. The tone of the article indicates a marginal preference for the immediate objective of capture rather than death.

Particulars of the Bhota amok case are just to hand, and, as will be seen, they are very gruesome. We are sorry to say the murderer still remains at large, but this is not due to any want of endeavour on the part of the police to capture him. District Inspector McKeon, of Kuala Kangsar, has relieved Mr. Conway in the hunt for this murderous brute, and we hope soon to hear of his capture, if he is not shot down like a dog, as he deserves to be. The man's name is Ngah Gafur, and he is between thirty-five and forty years old. He had not been living on good terms with his wife for a year past, and the latter, we believe, had been contemplating a divorce. This news, apparently has caused the man to go off his head, and commit the horrible butchery of his own flesh and blood. It appears on the afternoon of the 14th instant he left his house, where he has been living by himself, and went to his mother-in-law's, whence he removed his two children, both boys, aged seven and four, and took them to the house occupied by his wife close by. There a dispute took place between the husband and wife as to the future custody of the poor things, and it ended in the man seizing hold of one after another and cutting them down most ruthlessly; he then went for his wife, and, before the unfortunate creature could realise what had happened, despatched her after her children. The mother-in-law, who ran up to the assistance of her daughter, however, escaped with a deep cut on her shoulder; whilst the grandmother-in-law, a poor ancient dame, who heedlessly rushed shrieking to the scene, as fast as her tottering legs could convey her, was silenced for ever with two deep gashes on her neck. The blood he had already shed appears to have given the

amoker only zest to spill more, and his
next victim was his unhappy sister-in-
law, a young girl of about nine years or
so. Having thus disposed of his relations, he returned to his neighbors,
attacking a poor lone woman, and fatally
stabbing her with a spear, he inflicted
no less than six wounds on different
parts on the body of this woman. He
then proceeded towards Tronok, and at
about a mile and a half from the scene
of his first murders, and close to the
Tronok footpath, he came upon an old
man, who had taken up his residence in a
solitary hut in the jungle, to gather
the produce of a few durian trees he
owned there, and murdered him by stabbing him in the back, and he then burnt
down the hut. He also set fire to the
house in which his wife was living.
Gafur then . . . took to the wilds, and
has, as stated above, so far eluded a
party of the police, at first headed by
the Assistant-Commissioner and Inspector
Conway, and now under charge of Mr.
McKeon. He has, however, since burnt
down two more houses, and severely
wounded one of the Dyak constables now
scouring the country for him. One of
these asserts he had a passing sight of
him at about five hundred yards, and
this proves that the police are gaining
upon him, and that he will soon be
cornered.[17]

Case 4: Nyan

The case of Nyan, also reported by W. Gilmore
Ellis, bears much resemblance to that of Hadji
Ibrahim. According to the description, the sense of
rejection and loss of face generated by hearing
others speak disparagingly of him may be the triggering event causing Nyan to reflect, brood and,
after a period of time, willfully decide upon amok
as a course of action. It is interesting to note
that Nyan displays a degree of self-protective
rationality when he avoids engagement with an
individual bearing firearms. He seems at this point
and afterwards at least partially to regain sensi-
bility. He no longer attacks indiscriminately, but
rather attempts to flee.

49

It should be pointed out that Ellis, in his position as an official at the Government Asylum, probably dealt with an unrepresentative sample of amok-runners--those captured, adjudged insane, and placed in an institution. One should not conclude that this was an ordinary course of events in amok episodes.

Nyan came to Singapore on January 4th, 1890, four days before Amoking, with a party of traders from Brunei and Borneo, and all went to a lodging-house. On the evening of January 7th he went for a walk in a part of the town three miles from the lodging-house, and there met a man named Noor, whom he had never seen before, and after having a chat with him, asked to be allowed to sleep in his house that night, and this request was granted. On the morning of the 8th, Nyan returned to the lodging-house, Noor accompanying him; they went into an empty upstairs room, and Noor was giving a cigar and left by himself, Nyan entering an adjoining room, where were Awang and Mahomet, Bornean Malays, and members of his party. Awang was ill in bed, and Sleyman, his father, entering shortly afterwards, they all conversed amicably together. Nyan remained but a short time, leaving the room and going downstairs. He is supposed to have gone to an outhouse, where was his box, and obtained from it a kris and a parang. In the meantime, Mahomet also went downstairs, entered the eating-room and commenced to eat some fruit, and whilst he was sitting there, Nyan came in, and, without saying a word, cut at him, wounding him on the face and on the left forearm. Mahomet then fled upstairs, closely chased by Nyan, who succeeded in wounding him in the back as he jumped down a second staircase and got away. The Amoker now entered the room in which was Noor, attacked him, cut off his left hand at the wrist, and wounded him on the head and ear as the poor old fellow jumped out of the window into the street. Continuing the Amok, Nyan entered the room in which were Sleyman and his sick son, Awang. Sleyman promptly jumped out of the window, dislocating his ankle as he fell, and the body of Awang was afterwards found with the following wounds: Right hand cut off with the exception of a small portion of the skin, a cut at the back of the head going into the brain, a cut five inches long at the back of the right shoulder wounding the scapula, two stabs in the back, one penetrating the lung, a long cut on the left of the front of the chest going through the ribs into the pleural cavity, and a stab between the fourth and fifth ribs completely piercing the heart. After this ferocious attack, Nyan got out of a window on to the roof of some outhouses, and tried to enter the adjoining house through a window that he found open, but was prevented by a man inside with an old unloaded gun. He then got off the roof and out into the street, which he crossed. He then entered the sea, and was shortly afterwards arrested by a policeman in a boat, after first throwing both his kris and parang at his captor. None of his friends forming the party knew of any cause for the outbreak, and he had not quarrelled with any of them. Sleyman had known him for ten years as a quiet and industrious man. The ferocious attack on Awang could certainly be only the action of a madman, quiet and rational as Nyan was when I examined him but a short time after the occurrence. Nyan's story was that he overheard his friends say that he was not fit to live, and ought to die, so, getting frightened, he ran away and was kindly put up for the night by Noor. Coming back the following morning he again heard them speaking of him, and getting still more frightened he went for his weapons to protect himself, and then everything became red before his eyes and he can remember nothing more.

This man . . . has a quick, easily excited heart's action, and a peculiar stare in his eyes, which show much sclerotic, otherwise, although under observation for the last two years, I can discover nothing abnormal about him; certainly he does not appear to ever suffer from either visual or oral hallucinations. He is averse to being questioned as to the Amok, has a malignant expression, and his respirations become short, if so spoken to. He persists in the statement that after seeing everything red he remembers nothing until he found himself in the hands of the police. At his trial he was acquitted on the ground of insanity, and sentenced to be detained during her Majesty's pleasure.[18]

Case 5: Meng

The following account, probably fictional, merits attention not only because of the content of the episode, but also because its author, Hugh Clifford, was one of the keenest and most insightful European observers of things Malay. Again in a rural setting, the episode is of prolonged duration, with an attack by the amok-runner many hours after the initial foray. His wife is attacked first, then the King's Youths, and then, after some hours, random victims. Clearly there is motive and intent. In the absence of Europeans there seems no question about appropriate response; the amok-runner is killed.

Clifford poignantly depicts the utilization of amok as an ultimate form of individual rebellion invoked against the abuse of political authority. Indeed, some writers have thought the most prevalent etiology of amok to lie in response to the abuse of political authority and to the effects of oppressive political structures. While Clifford does not ardently espouse this position in other writings, he does in this case imply validity for such a motivational assessment. Of special interest in this account are the consequences of Meng's amok for his village.

They [King's youths] ate our substance, slaughtered our cattle for their food, stripped our fruit trees, and did us all manner of dishonour in the name of the King. But worst of all; they intruded into our households. Now a man's house

52

is intended by Allah to be his own; and a man's women-folk are dedicated to his peculiar service; but the naughty Youths, whom the King had sent for our defence, would by no means acquiesce in these proportions. Instead, they made love under our very eyes to all our women-kind--from the little virgin daughters, sitting secluded on the hanging-shelf, to the wife busy with her household affairs among the cooking-pots. It was a very great scandal, the more so since the fickle women,--for Allah hath withholden from these all judgment and discretion, dowering them only with a certain shame, that serves in some imperfect measure to curb the desire of their hearts,--flattered by the insolent attentions of these town-bred gallants, conspired with them unceasingly to work our dishonour.

One night when I was sleeping in my house in the village of Sega, I was aroused by a tapping on the door; and rising up, I beheld my brother Meng standing without, his face pale in the moonlight. At his bidding, I took my arms and went forth to join him; and then, with shaking voice, he whispered in mine ear how one Saiyid Ebong, a King's Youth, and a descendant of the Prophet Muhammad, had entered his house with four armed followers, and had bidden him roughly be gone. Now Meng, the son of my mother's brother, and therefore mine own brother to me, had been but lately wedded to a girl, the daughter of my father's sister's husband--a pretty maid, but sadly lack-ing both in propriety and discretion; and Meng wept with rage and jealousy as he thought of her closeted with the Saiyid. Yet what could he do? He was one man against four; he was unskilled in the use of weapons, and they were trained to arms from their youth upward. Moreover, they were of the number of the King's Youths, and under the King's protection. Therefore he had come to me, weeping and wailing, seeking my aid

53

and counsel. Together we aroused from
their slumbers sundry other of the
villagers, and told them that which had
befallen; but they were timorous, and
they besought Meng that he would make
with his calamity such issue as he
might, not involving them, lest some
worse trouble should fall upon the
entire village. I also added my prayer
to theirs; but Meng was past reason, for
the demon of jealousy had him in his
grip, and drawing his wood-knife--he had
no _kris_--he made as though he would have
slain me and then dashed from me in the
direction of his house. I followed at a
safe distance, and in the calm moonlight
I watched his figure flitting like a
shadow between the trunks of the cocoa-
nut trees. Creeping under the raised
flooring of his house, he stabbed upward
furiously in a certain spot, where he
knew the sleeping mats to lie stretched,
and a woman's scream answered the
thrust. I heard him give a hard cough-
ing cry, deep down in his throat, and
then he stabbed again, and yet again.
Lights sprang into red life within the
hut; there was a great outcry and commotion, a running to and fro of feet upon
the yielding bamboo laths. Then the
door was flung wide, and a knot of men
fell through the opening down the stair-
way to the ground. Meng dashed from
under the house yelling, "Amok! Amok!"
and flung himself upon the heap of
struggling men. I saw the blade of his
wood-knife rise and fall, flashing in
the moonlight; I heard cries of pain and
terror; and dimly, half revealed, I
spied the pale face of the Saiyid peep
through the open doorway and then with-
draw into the darkness.

I saw the struggling knot of human
beings break, just as a bubble breaks,
and become dissolved into its component
parts. The bodies of one man and one
old woman remained upon the spot over
which it had rolled and writhed. Meng's
weapon had taken so much toll. I saw
three figures rush away into the

shadows. I saw Meng, limping a little
from some hurt, and bewildered by the
darkness, run in pursuit, first of one,
then of another, and at last stand
still, his wood-knife dropping blood.
He raised a strained face skyward, and
the moonlight fell full upon it. Never
shall I forget that face! It was gashed
across by a cut from which the blood
flowed freely; the teeth were locked
together, like the teeth of a tiger that
has died fighting hard for life; the
skin was sallow and unpleasant to the
sight, as the skin of a corpse; and the
eyes, tense with agony and with despair,
were fixed accusingly upon High Heaven.
Thrice he cried aloud in a voice that
fell lamentably upon the quiet of the
night--cried to God: "Allah! Allah!
Allah!" It was a terrible cry to which
to listen, for there was in it a note of
great bitterness, a great despair, an
intense revolt against the cruelty, the
injustice of Fate. Then his voice broke
in a sob, and "Iang," he cried, and
again, "Iang, my little Iang," calling
pitifully upon his wife, for he knew
that he had killed her. Next, with a
sudden leap, he plunged into the brush-
wood at the edge of the village, and was
gone.

There was a great commotion in the
village, for word soon spread that Meng
. . . had run amok, and all doors were
barred and a strict watch kept. The
Saiyid, whose misdeeds had brought this
trouble upon us, was very angry, speaking pungent words to our elders, and
threatening them with the wrath of
Underneath-the-Foot, in that a gross
dishonour had been wrought upon his
servants. At dawn the next day there
was a panic at the river-brink, for
Meng, leaping from a hiding-place in the
underwood, fell upon those who had come
down to fetch water, slaying a man, a
woman, and two children, and escaping
unhurt ere any could stay him. At this
the anger of the Saiyid passed beyond
all bounds; and at last, obedient to his

bidding, we sallied forth, and Omar, the son of Chik, shot Meng from afar with one of the King's rifles while he sat dropping to sleep at the foot of a forest tree, not dreaming that anyone was at hand.

Later, when the Saiyid had made representation to the King, we of Sega were forced to pay much _diat_--blood-money--on account of the killings which Meng in his madness had wrought. _Ahi_, _Ahi_, that was, in truth, an evil season! Our crops were perforce neglected; we dared no longer resist the King's Youths, and could only shut our eyes, as best we might, to their wickednesses; and even when (longing to be free of these our oppressors) we rose and drove Wan Da and his people back into Selangor, the King sent one of his Treasurers up-stream, and exacted from our villages a heavy price as the cost of the weapons and the shooting-medicine which he had supplied, and which we had used for the routing of his enemies.[19]

Case 6: Man

One of the better documented cases of solitary amok is this account by John Gimlette, at the time Acting Residency Surgeon for Pahang. Man appears to discriminate in his choice of victims, aiming his aggression only at Chinese, but the quote attributed to Man immediately after attacking the Chinese--"I want to run amok"--indicates that fully indiscriminate homicide might have been forthcoming. As is common in amok cases, he is said to have been _sakit hati_, this "sickness" in Man's case apparently generated by past relationships with other Chinese. Gimlette finds no other source of motivation for Man's actions. Post-attack amnesia and paranoia amidst otherwise generally coherent and rational behavior, so often characteristic of the surviving amok-runner, are all present here. The post-episode hallucinatory paranoia is not mentioned in any other case reviewed in this investigation, suggesting the possibility of mental disorder or fever-induced delirium.

Man, a Mohammedan, aged about 23 years, male, a native of Kedah, single, was formerly in the Perak Police Force, but left the service when his time expired and came to Pahang, where he obtained work as a carter at Sempam.

About the end of last June [1900], Mr. Rance, his master noticed that he was odd in his manner. . . . For a few days he had been acting as a servant, but could not get on well with the others, who were all Chinese, He asked to leave on this account and was dis-charged.

Man came into Tras, a place near Sempam, where he spent two nights in the jungle, eating little or nothing, and apparently wandering about alone. . . .

He was not a ne'er-do-well, an opium smoker, nor a foolish extravagant Malay. He had no debts, no quarrel or love affair, but was evidently <u>sakit</u> <u>hati</u> with the Chinese. The words <u>sakit</u> <u>hati</u>, which form a phrase in common use among Malays, are defined in Marsden's <u>Dic-</u><u>tionary of the Malay Language</u> as resent-ment, malice, bearing a grudge. . . .

On July 6 Man came out of the jungle and went into a house at Tras where his native chief, Ismail, was staying. The house was empty at the time except for a Malay who was asleep. He took Ismail's sword from under his mat, went out by the back door and walked towards a Chinese shop in the village close by. Five Chinese and a Javanese coolie were sleeping and smoking opium in different rooms. It was mid-day, the men were strangers to Man. He slashed at the first two Chinese who were lying down and killed one, nearly striking his head off with the sword; he gave the other a severe wound on the face, which has since proved fatal.

Without uttering a cry he then diverged into a smaller room where two other Chinamen were lying down. He cut at one and brought him to his knees, killing his at once by a deep wound in the neck; the other man endeavoured to escape, but he wounded him on the arm and pursued him out of the door. The Javanese now seized him from behind and managed to drag the blade of the sword out of the hilt. It was loose. They struggled, Man fought and bit, crying out "I want to run amok." He finally "slipped away like a fish," to use a Javanese expression, and escaped almost naked into the village, where he armed himself with a large piece of timber. Several Sikh policemen forcibly arrested him, but he struggled so violently that he nearly broke away. At the inquest held the next day he could not be made to give any statement at all, but uttered a long continuous sort of whine. During the night he had done nothing but stamp and howl; the whole of Tras could hear him.

Two days later, the Assistant Commissioner of Police examined him in his cell. He talked in a friendly way, said he could not recollect the time spent in the jungle, and could remember nothing about the murders. He remarked that there were a few more orang kafir (non-Mohammedans) out of the world, and concluded that he must have killed them because he was charged with their murder by the Police. He ate rice, bathed and joked during the afternoon (July 8), but at midnight began to shout as if terrified, and was found crouching in the corner of his cell. He said it was full of people who wanted to kill him; he thought he saw them and begged to be taken out and tied up, if necessary, to a tree in the jungle. He quieted down and was brought into the Kuala Lipis Gaol.

Since admission, on July 13, he has been in a solitary cell, quiet, sulky and reserved, but quite coherent and apparently rational, except that his

58

memory of the murders seems to have been completely wiped out.

Man was certified as not insane by the surgeon in charge. . . .

Man is a well-developed Malay, apparently in good physical health. The knee-jerks are exaggerated; there is no history of syphilis. The urine is of low specific gravity--1006--does not contain sugar or albumen. . . . Vision is normal, but the pupils are equally dilated. His eyes are restless, the look being uneasy and the glance unsteady. I am not able to record any physical signs of insanity. There is no aural or nasal disease; the facial expression shows mobility. He persistently denies all memory of the amok, and has repudiated the acts which he has committed, so often, that I consider that he had no motive for the crime, and that this obliteration of memory is a genuine symptom of some phase of mental disease. . . .

There is no history of Man having had fits during childhood, and he has had none of the ordinary signs of epilepsy since he has been under observation.

At his trial, on October 8, 1900, he was judged to be insane chiefly on account of the fact that he had loss of memory, which, coupled with the previous history of delusion and hallucination, was sufficient to allow that he had been unconscious of his actions when he ran amok.

The demeanour of the prisoner in Court was curious--he was no longer depressed. His spirits seemed to rise and he was almost excited at times; he had loss of memory for names of places, and was evidently not alive to the fact that he was being tried for his life. He was transferred to the Selangor Asylum on November 29, 1900.[20]

59

Martial and Solitary Amok In Summation

Devoid of some of the twentieth century clinical imputation of physiological or psychological pathology, two nineteenth century definitions of amok in combination appear to best capture the many nuances of meaning resident in the term. First, in 1812 William Marsden declares "amuk" to mean "engaging furiously in battle; attacking with desperate resolution; rushing, in a state of frenzy, to the commission of indiscriminate murder; running a-muck. It is applied to any animal in a state of vicious rage."[21] In 1894 Hugh Clifford and Frank Swettenham define the term thusly: "Amok, to attack, to attack with fury, to make a charge, to assault furiously, to engage in furious conflict, to battle, to attack with desperate fury, to make an onslaught with the object of ruthless and indiscriminate slaughter, to run _amok_, to dash against, to rush against; an attack, an assault, a charge."[22] These neutrally-couched, generic treatments of amok encompass both the martial-collective and individualized-solitary forms.

This and the preceding chapter in part demonstrated that the two forms of amok were related in more than the fact that both possess the characteristics mentioned by Marsden and by Clifford and Swettenham. For in socially valued martial-collective amok lies the probable origin of solitary amok, over time fostering and reinforcing its occurrence and investing it with a degree of cultural legitimacy. It is not accidental that martial-collective and individualized-solitary forms are subsumed by the same general term--amok.

Chapter 4

SOLITARY AMOK: CHARACTERISTICS,
REACTIONS, AND TRENDS

Social Characteristics of the Amok-Runner

While available data do not permit definitiveness with respect to most of the social characteristics of the nineteenth and early twentieth century
solitary amok-runners, significant patterns of sex,
age, and locale of the amok incident can be
discerned. Probably the best-established fact is
that amok is strictly a male phenomenon. All
accounts are in agreement. There are apparently no
recorded instances of a female engaging in amok.

During the period under review, a Malay's age
was oftentimes a matter of speculation with exact
age usually of less moment to Malays than to
Europeans. In the many cases where the uprooted,
unattached urban amok-runner was killed during his
foray, there often was no way to determine age other
than by appearance. The conclusion to be arrived at
based on approximations and on cases where age is
recorded is that the majority of solitary amok-
runners were in the twenty to forty age range. In
any event, with life expectancy in the thirties for
much of the period, the pool of aged candidates for
amok was not great. The available evidence indicates that there were virtually none. The twenty to
forty age range among Malays is significant in that
it was during this period--as well as the late
teens--when the very limited opportunities for
upward social mobility were available. If a Malay
male was to be upwardly mobile during his lifetime,
it very likely would be due to his actions and the
events occurring about him during these years.

A matter of some importance is the rural-urban
dimension, both with regard to the residence of the
amok-runner and to the location of his foray. Here,
available evidence indicates that a majority of the
acts of solitary amok were committed in urban
settings by individuals who had been urban-dwellers

for only a short period. However, extreme caution must be exercised. First of all, the "urban" setting of nineteenth century Malaya was oftentimes little more than a very small village or town, usually at the mouth of a river or stream, often dominated by a sultan or chief and his followers, and characterized by a high degree of flux and impermanence. At any given time, many of these villages and towns, usually located on the seacoasts, were peopled in part by maritime transients from various parts of the Archipelago peripatetically engaged in shipping, trading, piracy, smuggling, or other maritime-related pursuits. Many amok forays were carried out by individuals from this population.

Most famous among these maritime transients were Buginese sailors from Macassar in the Celebes, present-day Sulawesi. The foremost sailors in the Archipelago, the Buginese, were known widely for their maritime and martial skills. During the eighteenth century, Buginese immigrants gained political ascendancy in much of the Malayan peninsula.[1] More than any other group, the Buginese Malays exhibited a proneness to solitary amok. Oxley, writing in 1849 as Medical Superintendent of Singapore and drawing on his experience with more than twenty cases of amok, states: "The Bugis . . . are by far the most addicted to the 'Amok.' I should think that three-fourths of all the cases I have seen have been by persons of this nation."[2] Ellis, writing in 1894, repeats this assertion: "The Bugis . . . are of all the Malay races by far the most addicted to the amok; in fact, nearly all amoks occurring in Singapore within recent times have been run by men of this tribe."[3] While these assertions may have been exaggerated, amok is often associated with the Buginese, presenting difficult analytical problems, since very little was usually known about the backgrounds and situations of the transient Buginese who ran amok.

While there is evidence demonstrating a disproportionate propensity toward amok among the Buginese, it is not valid to conclude that a substantial proportion of all cases of amok involved Buginese; these people simply happened to inhabit in disproportionate numbers those ports where European observers were likely to reside. For one must take into account that nearly all accounts of amok were recorded by Europeans, likely to be located in more urban areas and to be considerably less knowledge-able in reporting and analyzing rural events. With only a very limited written tradition among Malays, it is impossible to estimate accurately just how frequent amok may have been in rural areas which were relatively free of European contact. As will be reported later, native informants, in the nineteenth century believed amok to have been much more pervasive in the more rurally-dominated past. Regarding ethnicity, it is important that in these ethnically-heterogeneous societies, amok was almost exclusively engaged in by Malays. Apparently, neither Europeans nor Indians ever engaged in amok behavior, and there are only a few questionable reports of such behavior among the members of the large Chinese population. For the entire Malayan setting, only three cases identified by the original recorder as amok and perpetrated by non-Malays were discovered in this investigation. These three involved Chinese, and all of them manifested less than the full set of characteristics of the amok syndrome.[4] The ethnic exclusivity of amok within an ethnically heterogeneous setting implies that the phenomenon should be explained, at least in part, in terms of culture and social organization.

Having arrived at some very limited generalizations about the sex, age, residence, and ethnicity of those who commit amok, this analysis shifts to an intensive investigation of the amok episode. My approach is to divide the amok episode into three phases: the prelude, the attack, and societal reactions. Although using this "before, during, and after" scheme introduces an element of artificial compartmentalization into what is a single continuous process, this description will aid a subsequent exploration of etiology, patterns, and trends.

Prelude to Solitary Amok

We know very little about the intra- and inter-personal dynamics of the lives of most amok-runners prior to these violent episodes. Virtually without exception, their acquaintances indicated having no anticipation of amok (although in some cases ex post facto causal explanations were offered). Very little information came from the amok-runners themselves since, if they were not killed, they almost invariably manifested total amnesia for the entire episode.

In general, two basic patterns are discernible in the phase antecedent to amok. In the first, the individual displays behavior viewed as unusual but which apparently was not viewed as a precursor to amok.[5] The "unusual" behavior is generally reported as a several-day period of broodful sullenness. The period of brooding is reported to ensue in the wake of insult, misfortune, or undue oppression. Several writers portray well the feeling-tone of the brooding Malay, gradually building toward homicidal eruption. Best perhaps is the description by J. R. Logan:

> These amoks result from an idiosyncracy or peculiar temperament common amongst Malays, a temperament which all who have had much intercourse with them must have observed. . . . It consists in a proneness to chronic disease of feeling, resulting from a want of moral elasticity, which leaves the mind a prey to the pain of grief, until it is filled with a malignant gloom and despair, and the whole horizon of existence is overcast with blackness. . . . Whatever name we give the mental condition in which they are . . . it is clear that such a condition of mind is inconsistent with a regard for consequences. The pleasures of life have no attractions, and its pains no dread, for a man reduced to the gloomy despair and inward rage of the pengamo'?[6]

Central to the behavioral constellation is the feeling of sakit hati, the meaning of which is best expressed in English as "sickness of heart." Numerous authors comments on the incidence of sakit hati among nineteenth and early twentieth century Malays. Hugh Clifford describes the pattern as follows:

> By far the greater number of Malayan amok are the result . . . of . . . sakit hati. . . . The states of feelings which are denoted by this phrase are numerous, complex, and differ widely in degree, but they all imply some measure of grievance, anger, excitement, and mental irritation. In acute cases they attain to something very like despair. A Malay loses something that he values; he has a bad night in the gambling houses; his father dies or his mistress proves

64

unfaithful. Any one of these things causes him "sickness of liver."[7]

Ellis, from his position as Medical Superintendent of the Government Asylum in Singapore says:

> There is a peculiar condition of mind the Malay is liable to . . . in which he sits down and broods over his wrongs, or supposed wrongs, with revengeful feelings, to which the name of "<u>sakit-hati</u>" is given. Persons suffering from "<u>sakit-hati</u>" have been sent to this asylum. They do not appear to be really insane, and as a rule quickly recover. They remain in the condition for periods varying from a few hours to a few weeks, but rarely longer than four or five days. Their state is very similar to that of a bad-tempered child sulking and having occasional outbreaks of wrath. At these times their activity, especially of brian, is low, for it has frequently struck me that they have shown some slight impairment of memory when questioned afterwards as to what had occurred. . . . All Malays are subject to these attacks. Many have told me that the man who has run Amok always suffers from "<u>sakit-hati</u>" prior to his Amok, and I am of [the] opinion that careful examination of the Amoker shortly before his outbreak, were it possible, would invariably show divergencies from the man's usual habits, and in some cases marked peculiarities.[8]

Ellis's assertion that amok is always preceded by <u>sakit hati</u> or other noticeable behavioral changes is, however, questionable in light of a second general pattern of amok. In this second type of case, the amok behavior is reported to be a sudden, totally inexplicable outburst. With no warning whatsoever, almost as by startle reflex, an individual initiates frenzied indiscriminate homicidal behavior. In these cases there is apparently no <u>sakit hati</u>, no period of brooding, and no known grievances or animosities. The amok of Imam Mamat (reported in chapter one) and that of Hadji Ibrahim

65

(reported in chapter three) represent cases of this type.

Some reports of amok episodes give only the bare statistics of the case, usually name and residence of the perpetrator, location of the incident, names of those injured or killed, weapons used, and the immediate actions taken in response to the incident. These cases cannot properly be assigned to either category described above. While on the surface they might seem to fit the latter category, it seems fair to assume that in many cases the reporter of the incident simply did not have information on possible motives or on events preceding amok. Only when the reporter of an episode addressed himself specifically to events in the life of the amok-runner preceding the foray is it possible with any certainty to arrive at a conclusion regarding categorization.

The Amok Attack

The literature on amok consists mainly of descriptions of the attacks themselves. These accounts are often vividly detailed, and at a minimum they give the raw statistics of death and injury.

Probably the most remarkable characteristics of amok episodes are the suddenness with which they erupt and the largely indiscriminate aggression of the amok-runner. As mentioned previously, amok always comes as an unsettling surprise. There is no recorded instance of a correct prediction of solitary amok behavior by a given individual.

Little in the descriptions and analyses of solitary amok help us explain the sudden triggering of the attack. What is it that leads an individual, often after a long period of apparent contemplation, to initiate a solitary amok foray at a particular moment? The paucity of information in this area is due to the fact that the surviving amok-runner always steadfastly claims no recollection of any part of the foray.[9] He may recall events preceding the attack, for instance the period of depression and brooding if he experienced such, but there is never memory of the attack itself. He simply reports that he experienced <u>mata gelap</u> (lit., darkened eyes), what some Westerners might term "blacking out." While the imagery shifts between seeing black and seeing red, this is the last thing that he remembers. In some cases, he reports that he was surrounded by animals or demons and fought with them.[10] Ellis puts it succinctly:

> They remember that they were depressed, that they were upset, that they suffered from grief, in fact, that their affective nature was at fault. Many of them speak of having seen everything red, of having been giddy, or of their eyes having been turned inwards, but then comes the blank.[11]

According to Oxley, interviews with surviving amok-runners invariably lead to a response such as "the Devil entered into me, my eyes were darkened, I did not know what I was about."[12]

While the assertion is made repeatedly in the literature that the amok-runner is wholly indiscriminate in his acts of homicidal aggression, there is evidence in the episodes reviewed in this investigation of a degree of discrimination in the selection of victims, particularly in the initial stage of the amok foray.[13] Solitary amok usually begins with attacks against acquaintances of the amok-runner, often against close relatives, and even against members of a man's own nuclear family unit. Even amok attacks by the transient, unattached individual usually begin with aggression against individuals from the household where a man has been living, against his shipmates, or against his workmates. While it might be argued that this pattern is simply a function of the propinquity of these individuals to the amok-runner, it recurs to such an extent that it appears often to occur by intent, not chance. Whether or not the acquaintances victimized by the amok-runner are viewed by him as being responsible for his grief appears not to matter. Perhaps to signify the total seriousness of his intent and the overwhelming, irreversible despair he feels, the amok-runner often begins by attacking those individuals who know him best. Only infrequently are all his victims strangers to him. When he has attacked and, frequently, killed those with whom he has been socially and psychologically closest, the solitary amok-runner, like his martial counterpart, is then alone against the world. All are enemies. Indiscriminate aggression is the order of the day.

Thus there are faint indications that the amok runner discriminates in the choice of his initial victims; then, if he survives, he enters a state of full-scale frenzy and totally random homicidal aggression. If he is not taken before, the amok-runner is very likely to be killed or captured during this period. On some occasions he will confront and combat an individual attempting to halt his aggression; on other occasions he flees, apparently attempting to evade those who would kill or subdue him. There are several cases in which the amok-runner eludes his pursuers and escapes into the surrounding jungle (Imam Mamat in chapter one, Ngah Gafur in chapter three). The only recorded cases of this development indicate that the aggressive acts are continued, albeit with stealth and at a less dramatic, less frenzied pace. The amok-runner's aggressiveness appears to wax and wane, and his flight would appear to be an indication of an awareness that he is guilty of wrongdoing and that he faces dire consequences if overcome. It is still possible, however, that he may not be conscious of the fact that he has in fact wounded, maimed, and/or killed. There is no recorded instance of an amok-runner making good his escape, regaining his pre-amok equilibrium without outside restraint and assistance, and then returning to the area of his residence unaware of having engaged in acts of homicidal aggression. Whether his flight eventually results in death, in capture, in paying compensation so that he might return to his village, or in claim-ing the protection of a neighboring chief, it is not possible to discover if the amok-runner ever actually recalls his acts of aggression, other than through a simple acceptance of allegations made about him by others. It seems likely that in fleeing, intuitively or otherwise he simply does what he must do to survive.

Weaponry

The weapons used in amok forays are of some importance. With the exception of only one reported case,[14] the amok-runner unfailingly employs cutting, spearing, or chopping weapons.[15,16] Many authors note the extraordinary significance of weapons to the Malays and the distinct tradition-rooted passion for carrying arms. Clifford notes that in independent Malay states all men invariably went armed.[17] Swettenham, perhaps exaggerating somewhat, observes that "In 1874 every Malay had as many weapons as he could carry; say two daggers in his belt, two spears in his hand, a gun over his shoulder, and a long sword under his arm."[18] The noble as well as more pragmatic reasons for a Malay remaining constantly armed are discussed often in the literature. Newbold notes "Malays have a high sense of personal honour; and . . . the necessary weapons for avenging an insult are always carried about their persons, [thus] the outward deportment of natives to each other is remarkably punctilious and courteous."[19] Logan notes that the Malay is compelled to wear the _kris_ for the protection of his person and his honor and comes to view it as a part of his existence.[20] Galloway refers to the tendency among Malays to appeal to arms "the only 'court of appeals' known to his fathers for countless generations."[21]

Raffles mentions the prominence of the kris in Java as well as in the Malayan states and comments as follows:

> The custom of wearing the _kris_ among these islanders has, in its effects upon the manners of the people, proved in many respects an effectual substitute for dueling among Europeans. In these countries, where there is very little justice to be obtained from regularly established courts, and where an individual considers himself justified in taking the law into his own hands accordingly, the _Malayu_ is always prepared to avenge with the _kris_ the slightest insult on the spot; but the knowledge that such an immediate appeal is always at hand, prevents the necessity of its often being resorted to, an habitual politeness ensues, and it has been often said, that if the _Malayus_ are savages, they are by far the most polite savages that we know of.[22]

Gullick points to the high importance necessarily placed by Malays on arms during the constant warfare that plagued the Peninsula prior to and during the early period of British ascendancy. Fighting men used as many weapons as they were able to carry including the kris, _pedang_ (sword), _lembing_ (throwing spear), and _senapang_ (rifle or musket).[23] He also notes that it was the responsibility of the chief initiating military action to provide weapons, arms being closely associated with political power and weapons serving as an index of prestige.[24] Gullick provides additional examples demonstrating

69

the salience of sword and kris to individuals of
political authority:

> On appointment a chief was given a
> weapon, usually a sword, as a symbol of
> his office. When the Maharaja Lela
> publicly delegated authority to Pandak
> Indut he invested him with his sword. A
> sultan or a great chief sent out a
> herald with his sword as the symbol of
> his authority, e.g., for collecting tax
> or rounding up women. A Malay chief
> could marry a secondary wife by sending
> his dagger (keris) in token of his
> presence at the ceremony.[25]

As might be expected in such a context, a
substantial body of myths, legends, and magical
beliefs was associated with weapons, especially the
kris and the cannon, and there is much literature on
the subject.[26] Many of these beliefs centered on
the magical efficacy of weapons, and were aimed at
assuring invulnerability and victory.[27] Examples of
the magical infusion of desirable qualities to
weapons abound in Malayan literature and tradition,
making very clear the centrality of weapons to Malay
life.[28]
Thus, the choice of weapons by the amok-runner
is not surprising. Gimlette notes that "The intent
to kill is imperative and . . . the weapon used is
chosen with the idea of attaining this object
without fail. A stabbing or cutting weapon is
invariably used in preference to a club or firearm,
though . . . this may be due to the fact that they
are the national weapons and most likely to be at
hand."[29] Swettenham, writing in the 1890's,
observes that while the British had attained a large
degree of success in disarming the Malays, this did
not necessarily deter individuals bent on homicide.
"Nothing is easier than to obtain a weapon of some
sort, whenever it is really wanted, and as many
murders are committed, in this part of the world,
with a chopping-knife as with anything else."[30]
Thus, for reasons of availability, practical
utility, and cultural desirability, the amok-runner
relied solely, in the amok attack, on bladed,
cutting weapons.

Reactions to Solitary Amok

Societal reactions to solitary amok provide a number of clues that aid in understanding both its existence and its apparent decline over time. Such reactions are also important indicators of the etiology imputed to the acts of the amok-runner by individuals and groups in his environment. There are two alternative initial responses to amok: taking necessary steps to effect the swift and certain death of the amok-runner or attempting to restrain and capture him. In those cases where capture is effected, any of a number of secondary reactions may occur. For the amok-runner this meant being introduced into either a native or a Western system for the processing of dangerous individuals.

Sudden death was by far the most common fate of the amok-runner, his demise usually the culmination of a period of pursuit by villagers, townsmen, and/or police and military. In the cases reviewed, the amok-runner is speared or shot during the progress of his foray or in his attempt to escape; the wounds are often immediately or eventually fatal, and bystanders are sometimes ready to assure the death of the fallen amoker through clubbing or stabbing. According to a compendium of traditional Javanese law "_Amok_ being cried, it was lawful for every one to destroy such as ran _amok_."[31] According to the Code of Malacca "Persons running _amok_, be they slaves or debtors, should they not be apprehended, are to be put to death, and nothing farther [sic] said."[32] Whether motivated by a sense of self-protection, punitiveness, or by a genuine conviction that they were simply complying with the wishes of an individual preferring immediate death over life, the usual response by both Malay and Westerner was to employ weapons to halt as quickly as possible the advance of the amok-runner.

Numerous commentators assert that the usual reaction to amok was to as hastily as possible bring about the death of the amok-runner. According to Bird: "As his desire is to kill everybody, so, as he rushes on, everybody's desire is to kill him. . . . Usually . . . the fate of the "amok" runner is a violent death, and men feel no more scruple about killing him in his frenzy than they would about killing a man-eating tiger."[33] In a similar vein, McNair reports: "He is literally hunted down and destroyed, like a mad dog. . . . As the runner's desire is . . . to kill all he can, that of the peaceable is to slay him before he can do much mischief. . . . Generally speaking, the fate of the Amok runner is a violent death, few being reserved for trial."[34] These passages suggest that the amok-runner forces a life-and-death confrontation, turning everyday social situations into occasions for mortal combat. An interpersonal state of war is initiated by the amok-runner; others respond in kind. A facsimile of the dynamics of martial combat has been created.

At least until the latter quarter of the nineteenth century, there appears to have been little difference between Malays and Europeans with regard to whether the amok-runner should be killed or captured. Incentives for his capture alive did exist in both systems although this was usually precluded by the ferocity of the amok attack.

Other Malay Responses

With expedience and self-preservation dictating ready dispatch of the frenzied, homicidal amok-runner, what forces existed to lead either Malay or European to attempt to capture him alive? Elements in traditional Malay law provide some insight into this question as well as into the post-foray processing of the captured individual within Malay society.

Traditional Malay customary law, adat, is of two main types.[35] First is the mild indigenous matriarchal law of agricultural clans, the adat perpateh (law of ministers). Second, there is patriarchal law called adat temenggong (law of the minister for war and police). The composite adat temenggong contains traces of Malay indigenous patriarchal law as well as Hindu and Muslim law and was introduced largely from India, evolving as a means of social control for the mixed populations of ports. Under Malay rule, the adat varied greatly from one district or state to another, from one ruler to another, from one reign to another.[36] Our knowledge of Malay adat is based in part on digests of law and on tribal sayings. However, such digests and sayings are generally after-the-fact collections or portrayals of customary practices. The caution urged by Wilkinson is instructive and well-founded:

The first duty of the student is . . . to clearly understand the composite nature of Malay law. . . . He must not allow himself to be blinded by European preference for written or recorded laws.

72

He should not take the so-called "codes"
. . . too seriously. When he reads
about the "Malacca Code" or the "Malay
Maritime Code" or about the "Laws of
Bencoolen and Palembang," he has to
remember that these so-called "codes"
were never actually enacted by any
legislative authority; they are only
digests of Malay law. . . . A digest
. . . is . . . not the actual law--no
man can be charged in court with
violating some section or subsection of
a digest.[37]

Among many Malay groups, certain individuals
were in a position to benefit materially from fines
and compensation exacted from those guilty of wrongdoing or from related individuals. Malay adat
firmly established the institution of <u>bangun</u> (lit.,
to wake, lift up, restore) by which the wrongdoer or
those responsible for him gave restitutive compensation to those hurt by his acts.[38] The guiding
principle in the institution of bangun was restora-
tion of social equilibrium through provision of
compensation to those suffering injury or loss
through the acts of others, while at the same time
retaining wrongdoers as useful, fully-functioning
members of society. Crime was viewed as transgression against a family rather than the state.
Within the adat, where Hindu, Islamic, or Western
legal concepts had not intervened, the concept of
punishment for wrongdoing was largely absent. In
practice, inability to pay the designated compensation sometimes meant a period of debt bondage or
outright slavery for the wrongdoer or for an
individual or individuals held responsible for his
actions. Thus, in the compensation to be paid for
the death and injury inflicted by the amok-runner,
some individuals might have benefited materially.
These individuals would most likely have been the
consanguines of the dead of injured. In addition,
the <u>raja</u>, chief, or other rulers were likely to
benefit through payment of fines; indeed, such fines
constituted a major source of income for rulers.[39]
Since consanguines or others responsible for the
actions of the amok-runner could theoretically be
held responsible for compensatory payments,
incentives for material gain would not necessarily
dictate that he be taken alive, except for the
practice of outlawry, where those who normally would
have been responsible for an individual were

legitimately able to dissociate themselves from such responsibility.[40] In such cases the only prospects for obtaining compensation lay with the pengamok himself, thereby necessitating his live capture. This would have been especially so where the amok-runner was an unattached individual, perhaps transient and without ties in the area where he committed amok.

Where Hindu, Islamic, and Western legal concepts penetrated adat practice (especially adat temenggong), punitive responses such as death, mutilation, and imprisonment were commonly prescribed for criminal offenders. In most legal compilations we find varying admixtures of Malay, Hindu, Islamic, and Western legal concepts and practice. Interesting in this context is a Sumatran example provided by Marsden:

> A maxim, though not the practice, of their law, says "that he who is able to pay the bangun for murder, must satisfy the relations of the deceased; he who is unable, must suffer death." But the avarice of the relations prefers selling the body of the delinquent for what his slavery will fetch them (for such is the effect of imposing a penalty that cannot be paid) to the satisfaction of seeing the murder revenged by the public execution of a culprit of that mean description.[41] [Italics mine.]

Thus, even where the opportunity existed to punish a murderer by execution, the relatives of his victim or victims, perhaps encouraged by village officials who also stood to gain, apparently were more likely to opt for enslavement of the offender unable to make the bangun payment.

In the Malacca Code it is noted that should the amok-runner be apprehended alive, it is not lawful to kill him. "Should this be done [killing], and without the knowledge of the sovreign [sic] or his minister, the offender shall suffer death. For it is the usage that criminals when apprehended or bound, be considered as under the immediate protection of the sovreign, or his minister, in every part of the kingdom."[42] According to a Johore code, "Should the person running amok be wounded, apprehended, and afterwards put to death, the person so doing shall be fined one tahil and one paha. Should the amoker be grievously wounded and put to

74

death without the knowledge of the sovreign [sic], or his minister, the slayer shall defray the funeral expense."[43] Although the sources of these laws do not make clear for what reasons a sovereign might wish to have the captors stop short of inflicting death, one can speculate that it would be either for purposes of enslavement, collecting a fine, or in order to stage a formal execution. Windstedt points out that among many Malay peoples, a murderer could find sanctuary by making himself a slave of the Raja.[44] Ellis indicates that if an amok-runner "got successfully away and claimed the protection of his own or any neighbouring Rajah, he was at times taken by the Rajah as his slave. . . ."[45] This investigation came across no cases where this actually happened. Nevertheless, it is clear that those figures in power in a given locale often benefited materially from the levying of fines or from other actions taken against offenders and that the opportunity for benefits to accrue was heightened if the offender remained alive following his offense.

Based on the foregoing, it seems fair to conclude that in Malay adat there did exist certain incentives for effecting the live capture of the amok-runner. There is no way of knowing just how salient and telling such incentives were, and there is certainly little in the extant historical record to indicate that amok-runners were taken alive with any frequency in the traditional Malay setting. In summary, where Malay adat governed the response to the captured amok-runner, he faced at least one of the following: payment of compensation and/or fines, debt bondage, enslavement, or execution. It is important to note that if the amoker was bent on suicide, only the last of these possible outcomes eventuated in death.

Other Western Responses

Although their usual response was to inflict immediate death, Europeans at times sought to effect live captures of amok-runners. When capture occurred and the Europeans were in control of the area, the amok-runner was generally subjected to a Western interventive system for processing homicidal individuals. For the amoker this usually meant one of three outcomes: summary execution carried out with the intent of providing a deterrent; imposition of a death sentence arrived at after processing through Western-type courts; or incarceration and, possibly, treatment in a prison and/or insane asylum.

At least through the early part of the nineteenth century, European-inflicted or European-countenanced punishments for criminal transgression in Dutch Indonesia were extremely severe, often involving torture and mutilation.[46] During the latter part of the reign of the Dutch East India Company, the Dutch encouraged the capture of amok-runners. The reason seems to have been a desire to stage spectacular executions that would serve to deter future amok episodes. Police were provided with devices to restrain amok-runners.[47] In an editor's footnote in Stavorinus' Voyages to the East Indies is found a mention of an explicit material incentive being provided for a live capture: "At Batavia, if an officer take one of the amoks . . . alive, his reward is very considerable, but if he kill them, nothing is added to his usual pay. . . ."[48] If mortally wounded in the course of being captured, the amoker "is immediately broken alive upon the wheel, without any form of trial, in the presence of two or three of the counsellors of justice."[49] While not explicitly stated in the Stavorinus volume, it is reasonable to infer that execution in this fashion was also the lot of the amok-runner who was not wounded, although it is possible that a trial occurred between the time of capture and execution. Impalement was another method utilized to execute murderers or amok-runners.[50] That such severe punishments were intended as a deterrent appears to be the interpretation of the editor of the Stavorinus volume when he asserts:

> It is remarkable, that at Batavia, where the [amoks], when taken alive, are broken on the wheel, with every aggravation of punishment, that the most rigorous justice can inflict, the mucks yet happen in great frequency; whilst at Bencoolen [Sumatra], where they are executed in the most simple and expeditious manner, the offence is extremely rare.[51]

Given that only the barest rudiments of a formal judiciary existed,[52] such harsh penalties were probably commonly imposed in all those areas controlled by the Dutch East India Company.

The degree of success in efforts to capture the amok-runner alive during this period apparently was not high. The editor of the Stavorinus volume notes that "such is the fury of their desperation, that three out of four, are of necessity destroyed in the attempt to secure them."[53]

Reforms in judicial organization in Java came not only in the years immediately following the fall of the Company as the Dutch government assumed control but more especially during the 1811-1816 interregnum of the British in Indonesia under Raffles.[54] Raffles made substantial efforts to purge torture, mutilation, and other particularly severe punishment from the range of responses to those branded guilty of criminal activities.[55] He makes several interesting observations about the relation between the frequency of amok and the severity of punishments inflicted by the Dutch on wrongdoers.

> The [cases of amok] have happened exclusively in the large towns of Batavia, Semarang, and Surabaya, and have been confined almost entirely to the class of slaves. This phrenzy, as a crime against society, seems, if not to have originated under the Dutch, certainly to have been increased during their administration by the great severity of their punishments. For the slightest fault, a slave was punished with a severity which he dreaded as much as death; and with torture in all its horrid forms before his eyes, he often preferred to rush on death and vengeance.[56]

Thus, at least until the end of the hegemony of the Dutch East India Company in Indonesia, the Dutch response to amok appears always to have been death for the amok-runner, whether immediate or by means of staged execution. Unlike the native response which on occasion permitted the amoker to live, the early Dutch response left no question. He must die. Consequently, in areas under Dutch control where application of the severe punishment described above was operative, it appears that for anyone aware of these circumstances there would have been no incentive to attempt to survive the amok foray.

Following the reestablishment of Dutch control in Indonesia in 1816, the Dutch response to solitary amok and homicidal behavior in general is less clear-cut. It is known that substantial reforms occurred in judicial organization and that the Dutch retained jurisdiction in matters involving penal code violations, while leaving most civil matters to be decided by the native population according to the adat.[57] As the nineteenth century progressed, imposition of the death sentence for the survivors of amok or other homicidal acts seems to have become increasingly less common, while incarceration, long sentences at hard labor, and commitment to insane asylums became more usual. Changes in attitudes in Europe toward capital punishment appear to have had an impact on Europeans in Dutch Indonesia, so that the establishment of prisons and imposition of prison sentences for serious crimes gradually replaced capital punishment.

The establishment by the Europeans of insane asylums, particularly in the latter half of the nineteenth century, reflected what were viewed as increasingly humane attitudes toward mental illness and provided another alternative response to solitary amok.[58] However, not until the first quarter of the twentieth century does commitment to an insane asylum appear to become an accepted and oft-utilized response to surviving amok-runners. In 1922, Van Loon reports that asylums had been decidedly custodial in orientation, being used for incarcerating the most asocial and dangerous among the mentally ill.[59] Schoute provides corroboration here, writing as follows:

> No matter where . . . insane were received or whether they were Europeans or natives, at all events committing them to the establishment was nothing more than taking them into safe custody, particularly with a view to safeguarding the outside world. Nearly without exception, those native insane were very dangerous people, or murderers; quiet insane were mostly tolerated and supported by their family or neighbors in the kampongs."[60]

However, Van Loon reports that as late as 1915 it was not likely that individuals displaying the sharply aggressive confusion of the amok-runner would have been sent to an asylum. He explains thusly:

Patients, if they were aggressive in their confusion, usually were "laid down" . . . as amok-runners, and this mostly very thoroughly, as well by their fellow villagers as by the police or the military; or after a few days or weeks they either were alright again [and candidates for a judicial disposition of their case], or they had died, long before it was their turn to be admitted into an asylum; for the asylums in Java are always overfull. [Although] . . . more humane ideas with regard to lunacy gradually were spreading also in the Outer Provinces, everywhere in the Archipelago this line of conduct was followed, that the acutely alienated were locked up in the prisons, where very often they died, being without any nursing and treatment. . . . These last three years [1919-1922] these conditions have been considerably improved by opening the so-called Emergency-Asylums for the lunatic, into which now immediately all cases of sudden lunacy are admitted, so that opportunity of being admitted into an hospital is given to all Natives and Chinese, who suddenly go mad.[61]

In those instances where the amok-runner survived the amok foray, he might be incarcerated in an asylum, but probably only if he could first survive a prolonged waiting period in a most inhospitable prison. In other instances he was simply imprisoned. Without citing sources, Ralph Linton reports that in order to bring an end to amok, the Dutch eventually came to prescribe life sentences at hard labor for amok-runners.[62] That such penalties were utilized in cases where homicide was involved is noted in Bock's statement that in 1878 murderers and other criminals "were being sent from various localities in the Indian Ocean to expiate their crimes in the useful work of road-making, harbour-building, forest-clearing, and otherwise opening up the Dutch settlements in Sumatra."[63] Linton asserts that this form of punishment meant an "inglorious denouement" for the amok-runner thereby serving to rob amok of any glamour or heroicism that some might see vested in the practice. He implies that it was steady application of such punishments that led to the demise of amok. This current investigation, on the other hand, finds that no single factor is critical in accounting for the decline of amok. Furthermore, in the absence of any solid evidence to indicate that such a policy was consistently followed throughout the country or, indeed, that it ever existed to begin with, it seems quite reasonable to assume that at least some amok-runners probably continued to experience death, the penalty specified by the penal code for homicide.

Data on the nineteenth and twentieth century British response to solitary amok in the Straits Settlements and in the Malay states, especially from 1875 to 1925, is more substantial than that on the Dutch response in Indonesia during the same period. With the British relative latecomers to the region, there is virtually no data on British response to amok prior to 1800. Then, with the established British presence in the Straits Settlements, and with increased activity in the Malay states from about 1825 to 1874 culminating in the formation of the Federated Malay States and the Protected Malay States, the British found it necessary to deal with the pengamok. As with the Malays and the Dutch, the usual British response to mengamok was to kill the amok-runner during the progress of his foray. Nevertheless, prior to 1875, some amok-runners were captured alive in territory under British jurisdiction; after 1875, it appears that efforts were often made to capture them alive. Once capture occurred, a variety of responses were engendered, with an apparent trend toward increasingly defining the amok-runner as insane.

During the early years of their control in Malacca, the British apparently permitted the pre-existing Dutch judicial administration to continue. It is reported that in 1803 (eight years after the British takeover) an amok-runner in Malacca was tried in Dutch courts under Dutch laws, found guilty, and executed by means of crucifixion (probably impalement).[64]

In Raffle's 1823 proclamation to his successors at Singapore regarding the development of a constitution and laws for the Settlement, he provides guidance with respect to fixing a scale of punishments for criminal acts. He writes as follows:

> Severity of punishment defeats its own end, and the laws should in all cases be

so mild that no one may be deterred from
prosecuting a criminal by considerations
of humanity. No feeling interferes with
justice in behalf of a murderer, let
this crime be punished by death, and no
other.[65]

Exemplifying Raffles' attitudes regarding the
appropriate social response to homicide is his
action in the 1823 case of Syed Yassin reported in
chapter three. During the course of his amok, Syed
Yassin received mortal wounds. It will be recalled
that Raffles is said to have had the body placed in
a barred cage and suspended from a mast on public
view for a two-week period.[66]

Earl reports a case of amok in 1832 by a Bugis
sailor at Singapore who was subsequently tried at
the criminal court and acquitted on grounds of
insanity, perhaps a rather remarkable disposition
considering the time and place.[67] He was then
placed in confinement under the care of the colonial
surgeon.

In 1846 in Penang, the amok of Sunan is
attributed to his Muslim religion and he is
sentenced to be hanged, his body to be dissected and
the remains scattered about at the discretion of the
sheriff.[68] Ellis and Gimlette state that the
intemperateness of the actions of the judge subsequently became the object of considerable criticism,
but they provide no detail.[69] About 1850, Cameron
reports a case of amok where the amoker is stunned
by a blow from behind, taken prisoner, tried, and
hanged.[70] Buckley mentions a severe instance of
amok in 1863 by a Javanese sailor in Singapore.
While he was shot to death during the foray by a
British police officer, it is indicated that the
intent of the officer clearly had been to disable
rather than to kill.[71]

In the 1870's the British-based penal code for
the Straits Settlements and criminal procedure code
for the Federated Malay States refer only to murder
and assault, making no reference to amok.[72] Both
codes specify death as the punishment for anyone
committing murder, and amok-runners were often
treated as murderers. However, the Straits
Settlements Penal Code includes this statement:
"Culpable homicide is not murder if the offender,
whilst deprived of the power of self-control by
grave and sudden provocation, causes the death of
any other person by mistake or accident."[73] Thus,
an understanding that loss of self-control in the

face of "sudden and grave provocation" is to some
extent excusable might have guided judicial judgment
in some amok cases. In such cases (culpable
homicide not amounting to murder) the code specifies
penalties of penal servitude for life or imprisonment for up to ten years. These penalties parallel
those specified by the code of the Federated Malay
States.[74] The code also includes provisions that
excuse homicide in instances where an individual is
acting in self-defense or where a public servant, or
someone aiding a public servant, causes death by an
act thought necessary for the advancement of public
justice.[75] These provisions in effect meant that,
according to the law, death could be inflicted on an
amok-runner during the course of the foray with
little or no concern about subsequent legal
involvement.

The Criminal Procedure Code of the Federated
Malay States includes an interesting section on
procedures related to lunatics. Trials for criminal
acts could be postponed if it could be demonstrated
that the accused was of unsound mind.[76] If the case
was one where bail could not be taken (including
murder and culpable homicide not amounting to
murder), "the Court shall report the case to the
Resident, and the Resident may, in his discretion,
order the accused to be confined in a lunatic asylum
or other suitable place of safe custody."[77] Also,
"pending the order of the Resident the accused may
be committed to the civil prison for safe
custody."[78] Such an individual could be brought
before the court at any time and the trial reopened
if he was found to be capable of making his defense.
Upon a judgment of acquittal on grounds of lunacy,
it was required that the finding state whether or
not the individual had in fact committed the act in
question. If so, the Court "shall . . . order such
person to be kept in safe custody. . . ."[79] The
code made provision for official visits to such
incarcerated individuals, it being possible for the
Resident, upon the certification by the prison
inspectors or lunatic asylum visitors that an
individual was no longer of danger to himself or
others, to order them to be discharged.[80] He could
also order continued detention or transfer to an
asylum if the individual had been detained in
prison. While no similar section on lunacy appears
in the volume of laws and ordinances of the Straits
Settlements, the treatment of amok-runners in the
Settlements is evidence that very similar provisions
must have existed.

The Straits Settlements Penal Code was adopted intact for the unfederated (protected) state of Perak in 1884.[81] Similar action took place in the other states, so that by 1890 the above-described laws regarding homicide and lunacy obtained throughout the Settlements and the Peninsula.

In 1901, Gimlette writes that the only special reference to amok in any Western-based code applicable in territories under colonial domination was in the Indian Penal Code in a commentary to a section titled "Voluntarily causing hurt on provocation."[82] The commentary reads as follows:

> The meaning of this (Voluntarily causing hurt on provocation) and the following Section (Causing grievous hurt on provocation), of course is, that if a person who has received provocation assails the person who has given the provocation, he is only liable to a light punishment. But if, while out of temper on consequence of the provocation he were to attack an innocent person, or to run amuck generally like a Malay, the previous provocation would be no excuse.[83]

With the Indian Code adopted largely intact for use in British Malaya, it is probable that the reasoning evident in this commentary--to assail innocent individuals is inexcusable--doubtless guided judgments in cases of amok where insanity was not proven.

It is apparent that with British colonial domination firmly established in the last quarter of the nineteenth century, the cases of surviving amok-runners in British Malaya were increasingly processed by colonial courts. In 1878, McNair writes: "The object nowadays is to take the amok-runner alive, to try him by our laws, and punish him for murder."[84] In 1893 Ellis writes: "At the present time in the English States, and in all European protected native States and islands, an Amoker is arrested, if possible, and tried in the law courts for his crime."[85]

About the time Ellis writes, the available evidence points toward the frequent use of the asylum or simple confinement as two means of dealing with the captured amok-runner. The cases of Hadji Ibrahim (1887) and Nyan (1890) reported in chapter three both eventuate in acquittal on grounds of insanity and commitment to the conveniently available Government Asylum in Singapore.[86] In 1900, Man committed solitary amok in Pahang, was jailed for three months, tried and acquitted on grounds of insanity, and transferred to the Selangor Asylum (chapter three). However, during the same year, 1900, Gimlette reports that one Hadji Ali ran amok in Singapore, pleaded insanity at his trial, and was sentenced to death after having his plea rejected.[87] Shortly thereafter another trial was held for Hadji Sukor for a similar offense, and, "it is said, medical evidence on the state of the prisoner's mind was to the effect that nothing abnormal was noticed."[88] The final disposition of the case is not reported, although it seems safe to surmise that with no evidence of insanity Hadji Sukor received either a death sentence or a long term of imprisonment. Elsewhere, during the period of 1900-1920 in the unfederated Malay state of Kedah, one amok-runner regained his memory and his "normalcy" after one year in jail and was kept in detention for an additional four years and then discharged; a second was found insane and confined to prison, and he never spoke again.[89]

From 1890 through 1910, annual reports issued for the Straits Settlements, Federated Malay States, and the Protected Malay States (eventually the Unfederated Malay States) mention at least twelve cases identified as amok.[90] Capture and arrest occurred in seven of these cases while the amok-runner was slain or otherwise succumbed in the remaining cases. Unfortunately, in those instances where there was capture and arrest, there is usually no indication of the final disposition of the case. Following 1915 very few cases of amok are reported.

In sum, the general picture of the British response to amok during the period 1800 to 1925 is very mixed. The majority of amok-runners were killed or mortally wounded during the foray. Among those who were captured, some were found insane and incarcerated in prisons or asylums, some were simply imprisoned without being found insane, and still others were sentenced to death and executed as murderers.

However, with the establishment of colonial dominance first in the Settlements and then in the Peninsula, a western-based judiciary was organized, and it became standard practice to process amok-runners according to Western legal principles. With such a system to deal with criminals, the need to respond to cases of amok on an essentially ad hoc

84

basis was reduced (this is in contrast to the Dutch response in Indonesia during the rule of the Company). Incentives for the live capture of the amok-runner were generated, and the response to amok was less likely to be vigilante pursuit and severe summary justice. During the last quarter of the nineteenth century particularly, the responses of British courts to amok show a tendency toward defining the amok-runner as insane. The result was that civilian simulation of the complete martial amok scenario ending in death had become increasingly difficult.

Perhaps the most interesting trend, is the decreasing rates of the occurrence of solitary amok until a point was reached around 1925 when amok virtually disappeared as an identifiable, distinct phenomenon.

<u>Rate of Occurrence</u>

With only a very meager Malay historical record, a limited European record of most events and phenomena in the region before 1800, and a spotty post-1800 European record on the subject of amok, judgments are difficult with respect to the frequency with which amok occurred at any given time and with respect to trends in the rate over time. While in the post-1800 period the number of reports and descriptions of individual cases increases substantially, the evidence is decidedly insufficient to permit definitiveness in discussing incidence rates. In the final analysis, it is necessary to arrive at a judgment based on a review of apparently impressionistic, sometimes contradictory generalizations arrived at by various commentators.

Until about 1870, the comments of a number of observers indicate in very general terms that amok was a rather common occurrence. In 1811, Marsden reports that amok occurs frequently in some areas of the East, mentioning Java in particular.[91] It occurs with "great frequency" in Batavia and is "extremely rare" in Bencoolen (Sumatra).[92] In 1820, Crawfurd says solitary amok is "universal in the Indian islands.[93] In taking leave of Singapore in 1823, Raffles notes in a proclamation that it happens "often" throughout the area, going on to urge that laws be imposed prohibiting the carrying of arms and weapons.[94] In his 1846 ruling, Judge Norris asserts that amok is "frightfully common" among Malays.[95] In 1849, Oxley reports having dealt

85

with at least twenty different cases of amok where the amok-runner survived.[96] In 1869, Wallace notes that <u>mengamok</u> is common in Macassar (Celebes), stating that "there are said to be one or two a month on the average. . . ."[97]

After 1870, the majority of those writers discussing amok declare that, as compared with the time at which they write, the phenomenon was once much more prominent. In 1883, Bird states that "In Malacca . . . 'running amuck' was formerly very common."[98] At the same time she observes that amok "by now . . . is comparatively uncommon in these States [Peninsula]."[99] In 1893 Ellis, in authoring one of the more thorough and thoughtful investigations of amok, declares that "amok is far less frequent now than it was formerly."[100] In 1894, Clifford and Swettenham in their dictionary note that "amok running is becoming yearly more rare."[101] In 1900, Swettenham states that in the Straits Settlements amok attacks "have been exceedingly rare there; perhaps not more than three real cases in the last fifteen years."[102] He goes on to write "The Malay population has increased year by year, and yet, from being 'frightfully common' fifty years ago . . . the amok in the colony has almost ceased." Gimlette, Buckley, Van Loon, Galloway, Fitzgerald, Fletcher, and Yap all declare in general terms, without citing hard data, that over time the incidence of solitary amok dropped markedly.[103]

At least two commentators raise questions concerning the assertion that solitary amok was once a frequent occurrence. In 1837, Earl raises some question when he states that amok "is now almost obsolete; indeed it never prevailed to any extent except in those places in which the natives were oppressed beyond human endurance."[104] And then, many years later in 1922, Clifford states: "As a matter of fact, amok-running was not an event of very frequent occurrence, even in the lawless and unregenerate days."[105] While the preponderance of authors would seem not to agree with Clifford, it appears that the assertion that amok was once of "frequent" occurrence cannot be tested. No one other than Wallace specifies what is meant quantitatively by "often" or "frequent." It may be that Clifford's "not very frequent" refers to the same rate of incidence as does Marsden's "occurs frequently." What does surface from the present investigation, however, is that Europeans residing in the Archipelago and the Peninsula from 1800 to

1925 reported at least fifty-six cases identified as solitary amok.

It is possible that with Marsden writing in 1811 that solitary amok was of frequent occurrence and Crawfurd noting in 1820 that amok was universal in the area, these generally reliable observers initiated a myth that was accepted unquestioningly and perpetuated by succeeding authors. Trying to explain an isolated instance or two of amok, later authors may have simply accepted the early statements at face value and then gone on to note that the situation had changed, that amok was certainly no longer a "frequent" occurrence. Further, if one assumes Marsden and Crawfurd to have been in error, it is possible that some Europeans might have wanted to believe that these observations were correct.

Nevertheless, one important piece of evidence exists which appears to support the assertion that solitary amok did occur frequently at one time. This evidence lies in the existence of an interesting instrument said to be found in most native villages, the central purpose of which was to restrain amok-runners or other individuals engaged in aggressive use of cutting or striking weapons. It is described most comprehensively by Stavorinus, writing about Batavia in the latter quarter of the eighteenth century:

> In order, if possible, to take them [amok-runners] alive, the officers of justice are provided with a pole, ten or twelve feet in length, at the end of which there is a kind of fork, made of two pieces of wood, three feet long, which are furnished with sharp iron spikes; this is held before the wretched object of pursuit, who, in his frenzy, runs into it, and is thus taken prisoner.[106]

Ellis in 1893 states that

> From 60 to 100 years ago in all Malay states and islands long poles with prongs at their ends, shaped like pitchforks, were kept in the villages, and at the . . . cry of 'Amok! Amok!' were used by the inhabitants to pin the unfortunate Amoker to the ground if caught up from behind, or, if

approaching, to ward off his attack and keep him from coming near enough to use his weapon. . . . These prongs are to be seen in the more uncivilized parts of Malaya to this day.[107]

Raffles, McNair, Crawfurd and Bird also comment on the existence and use of this restraining device.[108] While it is not clear whether its origin is Malay or European, if its presence in the villages was as widespread as Ellis reports, it is clear that Malays considered the pronged pole an important device to have available, and this indicates that amok or amok-like behavior must have occurred with some frequency throughout the area at some time and that amok, as an actual or potential occurrence, was salient in the minds and lives of many Malay peoples. The presence of the restraining device in the rural villages and in the more uncivilized parts of Malaya indicates that solitary amok was not limited primarily to the ports and urban crossroads, for it is difficult to imagine such a pervasive presence of the device without its serving an utilitarian purpose. And the presence of the device throughout the Peninsula and Archipelago suggests that it was developed before the nineteenth century.

While the apparent gradual disappearance of the restraining device might also be seen as indicative of decreased occurrence of solitary amok, the advent of firearms serves to confound the equation. The rifle and pistol certainly offer more effective and less precarious means of halting the advance of the amok-runner. With Ellis' 1893 comment that the amok-restraining device can still be found in some of the more uncivilized parts of Malaya, he probably refers to areas of little interest to Europeans and little traveled by them. In such areas there would be a decreased likelihood of the presence of firearms and an increased proba- bility of the continued presence of the restraining device, an object perhaps technologically outdated in more advanced areas. The question becomes one of whether or not the availability of firearms to halt amok-runners is directly related to a decrease in the frequency of amok over time, or whether what appears to be a relationship is a spurious one. No final answer is possible, but it is plausible that the introduction of firearms, while playing a central role in the demise of military amok, contri- buted along with other factors to the decline of solitary amok as well. While amok had probably begun to become less frequent before firearms became pervasive, their advent could well have quickened the rate of decline.

Summary

The present chapter has presented and included discussion of data on the occurrence of solitary amok during the period 1800-1925 in the Malayan Peninsula and adjoining islands and throughout the Indonesian Archipelago. With regard to the social characteristics of the amok-runner, he is always male, usually between the ages of twenty and forty, and is often a transient resident of an urban area at the time of running amok, although probable reporting biases make conclusions on the variable of residence highly tenuous. Amok-runners were nearly always Malay with seafaring Buginese from Sulawesi disproportionately represented.

For purposes of analysis, the amok episode was divided into before, during, and after phases, and data was presented relating to each phase. Amok was never anticipated in advance of its occurrence although oftentimes is was preceded by a sullen broodfulness known as sakit hati. In other instances, amok simply erupted with no unusual behavior whatsoever preceding it. The attack phase of amok always occurred with dramatic suddenness. In the initial stages there may have been selective homicidal aggression against relatives or prior acquaintances which was then followed by indiscriminate aggression. The amok episode was always marked by mata gelap, amnesia, on the part of the amok-runner with regard to anything occurring during the attack. Due to availability, practical utility, and cultural desirability, bladed, cutting weapons were employed nearly universally by amok-runners.

A hasty infliction of death on the amok-runner was the most common response by Malay, Dutch, and British alike. However, restraint and capture occurred with some frequency, sometimes by design, sometimes not. Several features in the adat, customary Malay law, conduce toward restraint and capture, with certain categories of individuals, especially relatives of the deceased and rulers or their associates, deriving gain from the payment of compensation and/or fines, debt bondage, enslavement, or execution. Through the eighteenth century, the Dutch response to the captured amoker was most likely to be summary execution for murder, and it appears that in some instances incentives were offered to encourage capture so that spectacular executions could be staged for their supposed deterrent effects. In the nineteenth century, the Dutch were more likely to incarcerate the amok-runner at hard labor for life although some undoubtedly continued to be executed as murderers. Toward the end of the nineteenth century and during the first part of the twentieth century, the captured individual was increasingly incarcerated in custodial insane asylums.

Prior to 1875 in areas under British jurisdiction, the captured amoker was likely to face execution. By 1875, such cases were increasingly processed by colonial courts with simple confinement or commitment to an asylum frequent responses. While there was an increased tendency over time to define the amok-runner as insane the nature of the British response (as with the Dutch) was mixed. Some captured amok-runners were found insane and incarcerated in prison and/or custodial asylums, some were simply imprisoned without being found insane, while still others were executed as murderers. After 1915, very few cases of amok were reported.

Most writers after 1870 indicate that the rate of occurrence of solitary amok declined substantially over the years. The possibility exists that such assertions are simply the result of a colonially-created and perpetuated myth. However, the widespread existence among Malay peoples in the Peninsula and Archipelago of a device the central purpose of which was to restrain amok-runners, indicates that solitary amok may indeed have been rather frequent, quite widespread, and existing over a long period of time. On balance, the evidence generally supports the assertion that the frequency of solitary amok declined.

Chapter 5

SOLITARY AMOK: AN ETIOLOGICAL
REVIEW AND DISCUSSION

Etiological Factors in Solitary Amok

In trying to account for the occurrence of
solitary amok, many early authors and analysts
posited single factor explanations of the phenomenon. In most instances, cases labeled amok were
cited which lent support to the arguments being
proffered. In other instances no data were presented, and the arguments or analyses amounted to
nothing more than ideologically-based pro-Western or
anti-Muslim diatribes. To the former group belong
those analyses which focused on the consumption of
opium, hemp or other such substances as well as
those which viewed amok as a disease-induced
delirium. In the latter group, at least for
Malaysia and Indonesia, belong those analyses which
cited Muslim beliefs and traditions as the sole
causative factors, as well as those which viewed
amok as an expression of a primitive, uncivilized
psyche. However, from time to time, some authors
emphasized convincingly the importance of sociogenic
and psychogenic factors in the occurrence of
solitary amok, and it is to these factors that the
present analysis ultimately turns.

Drug Intoxication

Perhaps the most frequently tendered explanation for the occurrence of amok has been that it
stems from the use of opium or hemp (Cannabis sativa
or Cannabis indica). While there have been studies
linking amok-like behavior to the use of toxic
mushrooms among Norse warriors and in new Guinea,
these behaviors bear only symptomatic similarities
to amok, for amok is rooted in a sociogenic-
psychogenic base.[1]
Nowhere did this investigation reveal even
moderately convincing evidence that the use of opium

in itself could lead to the display of amok symptomatology; those accounts purporting such to be the case simply assume such etiology as a given.[2] But while opium consumption was indeed common in Indonesia and Malaysia during the period of this analysis, the physiological effects of opium are anything but violent, frenzied aggression. Indeed, quite the opposite is true. Probably the most telling argument against the position that amok is generated by opium use lies in the absence of amok or amok-like behavior among the large Chinese population in this region, the Chinese being the most inveterate users of opium. Cameron in 1865 notes that "Some have written that they [amok cases] most generally arise from the dejection succeeding an over-indulgence in opium. But the Malays are seldom addicted to the use of that drug, and nearly all the amoks that have occurred in Singapore were run by men who had never tasted it."[3] In focusing on opium as the sole or primary etiological factor in the occurrence of amok, these Western observers appear to have simply seized on a favorite Western whipping-boy.[4] Marsden puts it well:

> It has been usual also to attribute to the practice [opium use], destructive consequences of another nature; from the frenzy it has been supposed to excite in those who take it in quantities. But this should probably rank with the many errors that mankind have been led into, by travellers addicted to the marvellous; and there is every reason to believe, that the furious quarrels, desperate assassinations, and sanguinary attacks, which the use of opium is said to give birth to, are idle notions, originally adopted through ignorance, and since maintained, from the mere want of investigation, without having any solid foundation.[5]

The link between consumption of hemp derivatives and amok-like behavior is much better established and deserving of more detailed attention. It was common for British physicians in nineteenth and early twentieth century India to ascribe to the use of hemp acute confusional disorders in general and cases of amok in particular. Chevers, in his impressive volume on forensic medicine in India, gleans from court reports a number of cases involving amok symptoms, and the majority of these cases note that the disturbed individual was a user of one of the hemp derivatives, sometimes with evidence presented that he had been smoking or consuming the drug immediately prior to the attack.[6] In some cases the claim is made by the accused that he was under the influence of hemp when the attack occurred, apparently in the attempt to explain and excuse his behavior. Intoxication caused by use of ganja, bhang, or hashish (called charas in India) is usually cited. Chevers also cites several amok-like episodes where there is no evidence of any such use by the accused. Chevers concludes as follows:

> I am convinced that a very large propor-
> tion of the murders by hacking to pieces
> . . . are committed under the influence
> of intoxicating drugs. . . . It is a
> matter of popular notoriety, both in
> Bengal and in the North Western
> Provinces, that persons intoxicated with
> ganja are liable to commit acts of
> homicidal violence. . . . The most
> singular feature in this class of cases,
> is the impulse which, almost invariably,
> urges the prisoners, after having
> satiated their vengeance, to continue
> their havoc upon unoffending persons.
> It is evident that no peculiar opinions
> of religion, or custom, or class can
> prevail in these cases; for we find the
> crime perpetrated, under precisely
> similar circumstances, by the upcountry
> Rajpoot, the Bengalee, the Ooriah, the
> Mugh of Arrakan, and the Malay of
> Singapore. All that these men can be
> said to have in common is that their
> natures are revengeful, that they live
> under a tropical sun, and are habituated
> to excess in the use of intoxicating
> drugs. Carefully sifted, it is probable
> that the generality of these cases would
> be found to be dependent upon the last-
> mentioned fact.[7]

In 1921, A. W. Overbeck-Wright, in Lunacy in India, views Cannabis indica as a direct etiological factor in amok. According to Overbeck-Wright:

> The patient as a rule broods over some
> fancied wrong until life becomes unbear-

93

able, and he determines to end it. With
this object in view he has recourse to
drugs, with the object of inducing a
state of frenzy and in most cases
Cannabis Indica is the one chosen. When
absolutely beside himself with the
effect of the poison, he seizes his
weapon and rushes blindly forth, cutting
and hacking at everyone he sees, killing
or maiming all he meets, until a timely
bullet or sword cut puts an end to the
slaughter by causing his death.[8]

Overbeck-Wright appears to have combined language
from various efforts to describe amok among Malays
with his belief that consumption of Cannabis indica
is usually a purposeful precursor to amok. In his
view, amok is an intentional act with the use of
Cannabis indica an expedient to engagement in such
behavior.
        A 1930 article by Dhunjibhoy provides a
detailed description of a syndrome designated
"Indian hemp insanity" and is of particular
interest.[9] Indian hemp insanity is described as a
mental disease produced by excessive or prolonged
moderate use of hemp. It occurs primarily in males
aged twenty to forty and includes delusions,
hallucinations, increased psychomotor activity,
tendency to wilful damage and violence, followed by
deep sleep and forgetfulness of all but the initial
symptoms. The symptomatology is virtually identical
to that seen in many cases of amok. Dhunjibhoy
comments that "I shall not hesitate to believe
anyone who commits acts of violence under the
influence of drugs and pleads complete amnesia of
the crime on recovery."[10] He notes that cases of
hemp insanity were common in India and nearly always
manifested the full range of symptoms mentioned
above.
        With hemp derivatives in use at least during
the nineteenth century, it is probable that some of
the cases termed amok in Malaysia and Indonesia
involved hemp consumption immediately prior to the
episode. If the Dhunjibhoy and Chevers analyses of
the relationship between hemp use and violent
behavior are accurate, it may be that hemp
derivatives were utilized by Malays in some cases to
generate amok behavior intentionally as stated by
Overbeck-Wright while in other cases violent
behavior may have been an unintentioned consequence
of prolonged hemp consumption. However, the fact

94

remains that for a decided majority of the cases designated as amok in Malaysia and Indonesia, there is no indication that drug intoxication, hemp or otherwise, is involved.

Marsden, writing at the beginning of the nineteenth century, makes a number of important observations about the relationship of amok and hemp consumption. Marsden writes the following:

> It is not to be controverted, that these desperate acts of indiscriminate murder, called by us, mucks, . . . do actually take place, . . . but it is not equally evident that they proceed from any intoxication, except that of their unruly passions. . . . It is true that the Malays, when in a state of war they are bent on any daring enterprize, fortify themselves with a few whiffs of opium, to render them insensible to danger; as the people of another nation are said to take a dram for the same purpose; but it must be observed, that the resolution for the act precedes, and is not the effect of the intoxication. . . . Upon the whole, it may be reasonably concluded, that the sanguinary achievements, for which the Malays have been famous . . . are more justly to be attributed to the natural ferocity of their disposition, or to the influence upon their manners of a particular state of society, than to the qualities of any drug whatever.[11] [Italics mine.]

In sum, while the use of hemp may have been an important etiological factor in at least some of the cases that were labeled amok in Malaysia and Indonesia, its use appears unrelated to the large majority of cases reviewed in this analysis. Only where amok behavior was an accidental unintentioned consequence of the use of hemp (Indian hemp insanity) do we find a basis for a challenge to the sociogenic-psychogenic-based category of solitary amok developed below. In those cases where hemp was used purposely to generate amok behavior, Overbeck-Wright indicates and Marsden would probably concur that the resolution for the act of amok preceded the use of the drug and that the act of amok itself, sociogenically and psychogenically rooted, was central in the thoughts of the user. Drug use and intoxication may account for some cases of amok-like behavior that because of symptomatic similarity with amok were labeled amok, but in general they appear to be of limited explanatory value for the universe of amok cases in Malaysia and Indonesia.

Epilepsy

Several observers have commented on the similarities between running amok and some types of epileptic seizure. Foremost among these was Kraepelin who, during a stay in Java at the beginning of the twentieth century, classified amok as an epileptic dream-state.[12] Fitzgerald describes a number of "epileptic equivalents" in amok episodes: "Epilepsy with its preparoxysmal stage, its aurae, often visual; amok with its preparoxysmal stage and visual aurae."[13] According to Gimlette:

> The mental upheaval of amok has some of the clinical features of epileptic mania. There is impulsiveness, violence, homicide, and destructiveness. It seems to resemble also very closely the automatic condition left after an epileptic fit, more particularly the so-called 'procursive' or 'procursine' epilepsy, in which the patient starts to run. The red vision, or field of blood . . . is also significant of an epileptic aura, but there seem to be no motor or visceral aurae.[14]

Van Loon, working in the same institution at Buitenzorg (Bogor) where Kraepelin arrived at his conclusions, challenges Kraepelin directly, stating that "it is obvious that epilepsy, if at all playing a part as a cause of . . . amok . . . is of only a minor importance."[15] Elsewhere he states that "undoubtedly the great majority of cases of amok is not caused by epilepsy. Of the fairly large number of epileptics we could observe in the Indies . . . not a single one ran amok."[16] Writing in 1938, Fletcher is explicit: "There is no case on record of typical amok in a Malay which was due to epilepsy."[17] In general while there do exist some similarities in amok and epileptic behavioral manifestations, this investigation has discovered no convincing evidence of direct linkage between the two phenomena.

Malarial and Other Physiological Infection

Several authors have observed the similarity between running amok and the aggressive behavior occasionally manifested by individuals experiencing or who have recently experienced malarial or other infection-induced fever. In 1924 Fitzgerald reported that "in the Johore gaol the last six persons admitted . . . for running amok were found to be suffering from malaria fever, in all cases the quartan parasite being demonstrated."[18] He was inclined to designate malaria as one of a list of exciting causes. At about the same time, Van Loon reported that individuals sent to the Buitenzorg asylum as amok-runners were often found to have malaria, sometimes combined with syphilis, and he concluded that these and other infections accounted for the vast majority of amok-like aggressive behavioral manifestations exhibited by such individuals.[19] Galloway describes post-febrile insanity, usually following malaria, but also known to follow dengue, the paratyphoids, and other non-malarial fevers.[20] He states that the maniacal form of post-febrile insanity closely resembles amok.

> The records of any tropical asylum will show how very frequently on admission a history of a previous febrile attack is given, and naturally on account of its numerical preponderance malaria is the most common cause. . . . The more one hears of amok cases, the more closely the immediately previous history is inquired into, the more will it be brought home that post-febrile insanity as a cause of amok is by no means infrequent.[21]

Fletcher concludes that it is probable that the depression following malaria is a factor in some cases designated as amok[22] and, on balance, the evidence does appear to suggest the existence of a physiological infectious origin for a small proportion of amok episodes.

It must be emphasized that there exist numerous descriptions of amok episodes where there is no mention of physiological infection, either at the time of or preceding the episode, and where it appears that the amok-runner was fully sane and healthy up to the moment of the attack. Furthermore, evidence has been cited which indicates that

97

the incidence of amok was very much on the wane by the turn of the nineteenth century; yet, major inroads in decreasing the incidence of infectious diseases in Malaysia and Indonesia were not made until the second quarter of the twentieth century. If the etiology of amok lies primarily in physiological infection, one would be hard put to account for the apparent decrease in the occurrence of amok well in advance of decreases in the rate of occurrence of the infectious diseases. Furthermore, the Chinese and other resident groups were as susceptible to such infections as anyone else, yet they do not run amok. In sum, it is justifiable to conclude that delirium induced by physiological infection provides the vehicle for some cases of amok behavior, and this conclusion forms the primary basis for one of the categories of solitary amok developed below.

The Influence of Islam

In the late thirteenth century Marco Polo found Islam established on the northeast coast of Sumatra. Available evidence indicates that Islam was initially introduced into Malay regions by Muslim missionaries from the Coromandel coast of southern India. Early in the fifteenth century the rulers of Malacca embraced Islam. It was then spread throughout the region by traders who came to trade in the ports of the area and by individual men of religion, some of whom came at the invitation of the local potentates.[23] Islam was carried to Java, Borneo, and other islands until the majority of the peoples of greater Malaysia became orthodox Muslims of the school of Shari'a. Although relics of animism and shamanism remain dominant in some remoter areas to this day, in most areas varying Islam-Hindu-Animist syncretic constellations characterize Malaya religious beliefs and practices.

With Islam decidedly the dominant religious force in the area, some observers have found factors in Muslim beliefs and practices that they think explains the occurrence of amok among Malays. Perhaps the most elaborate statement of such thinking lies in the previously-cited remarks of Sir William Norris in sentencing the amok-runner Sunan (chapter three). Others have cited the existence within Islam, of a sanctioned tradition of fanaticism as well as strict prohibitions against suicide as being factors contributing to the occurrence of amok. Probably what these observers had in mind is summarized by Ewing in his discussion of juramentado, religiously-influenced fanatical aggressive frenzy among the Muslim Moros of the Philippines.

In juramentado, highly ritualized preparations precede the homicidal phase. Then 234366.

> after arriving at the place he has selected for his execution of Christians, [the person] grasps his weapon . . . and attacks any Christians available. The first time he strikes a victim, he shouts "Bismallah" (In the name of God); but he does not repeat this when striking subsequent victims. If he approaches a Mohammedan or a group of Mohammedans, he warns them off by shouting "Simay Islam" (Mohammedans keep clear). His intention is to kill as many Christians as possible. Such is the frenzy of these juramentados that they sustain many wounds before succumbing. The people seek sanctuary in a Church, or wherever possible.

> After his death, the juramentado believes, he will mount a flying horse . . . which will bear him to Heaven, where forty houris . . . are waiting to be his wives. In Heaven, too, there are all the best foods he can imagine . . . ; there is no need of ever doing any work; the surroundings are of the greatest possible beauty.

> Suicide is forbidden the Moro, but this manner of ending one's life is highly esteemed. It is "going out like a man."[24]

Ewing does not doubt that juramentado has a pronounced religious element in its motivation. Of importance is the fact that the Koran calls one a martyr who succumbs in a battle during the jihad (holy war) after having killed some of the enemy. Ewing states: "In the case of the historical juramentados who attacked the enemy with frenzy during time of war, the purely religious element in motivation was no doubt much larger than in the case of the individual juramentado of today."[25] He concludes that juramentado in more recent times constitutes an institutionalized mode of suicide among the Moros, a pattern of behavior clearly influenced by Muslim teaching, as adopted and adapted by the Moros.[26]

While most observers agree on the historical importance of the religious influence in the juramentado of the Moro, a number of the more thoughtful writers on the topic of amok challenge the assertion that Muslim belief and practice is a directly related influence amongst the Malays of Malaysia and Indonesia. Ellis is relatively thorough on the matter:

> Sir William Norris seems to have been under the impression that Amok has something to do with Mahomedanism, that the murder of infidels (i.e., non-Mahomedans) is advocated, or at least spoken well of in the Koran, and that to be killed while running Amok is a sure road to heaven. To this day this is frequently put forward by some European residents as the real reason for commit-ting Amok. Never was there a greater error; Amok is a peculiarity of the Malay race, and the fact of their . . . being Mahomedans has really nothing to do with it. As to the Koran, I have studiously searched through it for anything bearing on the point, and can find nothing, and questioning educated Malays has given the same result. . . . Moreover, a Malay is no respecter of persons when Amoking, and he stabs members of his own race and religion, should he come across them, with the same indifference with which he would stab others, an action he would certainly not commit were the Koran or his religion in any way the cause of the outbreak. Concerning such a crime the Koran says: "But whoso killeth a believer designedly his reward shall be hell, he shall remain therein for ever, and God shall be angry with him, and shall curse him, and shall prepare for him a great punishment. . . ."

> Many Malays have told me that they consider Amok a kind of suicide; a man, from some cause or other, considers life

not worth living, and wishes to die--
suicide is a most heinous sin according
to the ethics of the Mahomedan reli-
gions, therefore he Amoks, in the hope
of being killed. Concerning the crime
of suicide, the Koran says--"Neither
slay your selves, for God is merciful
towards you, and whoever does this
maliciously and wickedly he will surely
cast him to be broiled in hell fire; and
this is easy with God." Suicide is
extremely rare amongst Malays and only
one attempt has ever been brought to my
notice. . . .[27]

Toward the end of the eighteenth century
Crawfurd writes that "the natives of the Eastern
islands ran a-muck before they ever heard of the
Muhammadan religion, and the unconverted natives at
the present day equally run a-muck with the
converted."[28] Elsewhere, Gimlette writes:

The well-known association of suicidal
mania with religious melancholia seems
to have led other observers to conclude
that the influence of the Mohammedan
religion may be a factor in the causa-
tion. But although amok has made the
Malays and their descendants notorious
all over the world, it does not appear
to have affected the millions of
Musselmans in Turkey, and most other
Mohamedan countries. The victims
generally fall quite independently of
creed, nationality, or relationship.
And, although a good deal of religious
fanaticism may be induced in the melee,
I do not think from what I know of
Pahang Malays that the pure Mohammedan
religion has anything to do with amok.

As far as the unpremeditated murders
of amok go I think that the laws of the
Koran relating to murder clearly support
[this] opinion. . . . I doubt whether
the ordinary Pahang villager has ever
studied these laws, but the question
seems to be of little importance,
because doubtless Malays have been
carried away by the blind passion of
amok long before the comparatively

101

modern conversion of the race to
Mohammedanism.[29]

On balance there is an absence of convincing
evidence that support within Islam for fanatic
aggression against non-Muslims explains the
occurrence of amok among Malay peoples. Such a
conclusion appears warranted by the lack of
religious-based discrimination in the selection of
victims and also by the fact that amok amongst
Malays apparently preceded the widespread introduction of Islam and was engaged in by non-Muslim as
well as Muslim Malays. At most, it may be that the
Muslim institution of the jihad and the apparent
attendant supports for fanaticism in the military
context may have served to reinforce indigenous
traditions of martial amok in southern India and in
the Malay regions. To the extent that this is true,
Islam then could also be viewed as of indirect
influence in the genesis of solitary amok, since it
appears likely that the occurrence of solitary amok
among Malays flows out of the honored existence of
such behavior in the martial context. In contrast
to the case of juramentado among Filipino Muslims,
this investigation has revealed no data to suggest a
stronger link than this between Muslim supports for
fanatic aggression and the occurrence of amok in
Malaysia and Indonesia.

As for strong Muslim strictures against
suicide, here again it appears appropriate to view
this facet of Islam as a reinforcing element in the
total cultural-institutional base, but probably not
in itself a primary etiological factor. Apparently
the Malay disinclination to suicide is of long
standing and did not originate with the advent of
Islam. Although some cases of solitary amok may
have been generated out of a wish to commit suicide,
it does not follow that Muslim proscriptions against
suicide in themselves led to the choice of amok as
an alternative preferable to self-inflicted death.
Such proscriptions may have been part of the
overarching constellation of factors indirectly
contributing to the occurrence of amok, but probably
were rarely, if ever, of central etiological
significance in themselves.

Primitive Mentality

Several observers have argued that the violent
aggression and fury of amok is simply the product of
a primitive, uncivilized psyche. Van Loon in 1927

claims that the psychic structures of the Malay and Westerner differ in that the Malay is susceptible to being inundated by affects, or strong feelings, with the result that "all counter-motives and checks are wiped away, and the affect completely rules thought and action."[30] Van Loon continues:

> In this respect (as in many others) all primitive races resemble very much the psyche of children, . . . [with] imperfect control of affects. . . . The higher a people (or individual) is civilized, the better it learns to control its affective reaction. . . . The peculiar psychic nature of the Malay is responsible for the symptoms which render this syndrome [amok] entirely different from similar ones in Europe.[31]

Writing at about the same time as Van Loon, Galloway speaks of the absence of "civilized" inhibitions among "untutored races" such as the Malays. He writes as follows:

> The impress of the primitive mind lies broad over the whole series of events; the inflated self-esteem, the proportionate resentment at the wounding of it, the tendency of the resentment to pass uninhibited into action against the offender, the necessity of re-establishing his prestige in the eyes of his fellowmen, the appeal to arms--the only "court of appeal" known to his fathers for countless generations.[32]

Elsewhere, Galloway speaks of a strong "instinct of pugnacity" and the resort to weapons an "instinctive act."[33]
     Assignment of causal significance to race as such or to instinct is always dubious and would be found credible by few, if any, present-day analysts. As Yap notes, "It is a mistake to equate deficient powers of inhibition as such with so-called primitiveness."[34] As is usual with such explanations, there is no convincing data to support them, and the observations of Van Loon and Galloway are appropriately assigned to the realm of speculation.

103

Solitary Amok: An Etiological Classification

All of the purported etiologically-relevant factors thus far reviewed, whether singly or in combination, fall short of providing a satisfactory explanation of the amok phenomenon and trends in the rate of its occurrence. Drug intoxication, physiological infection, and Islam are of some etiological importance, but a comprehensive explanation requires attention to an interrelated complex of social, cultural, and historical factors. Furthermore, it is evident that the various commentators on solitary amok were not all writing about exactly the same phenomenon, and a basic classificatory distinction is helpful for better understanding the causes of amok.

Fundamental to the occurrence of any form of solitary amok is the culturally-conditioned nature of amok behavior and the quasi-legitimacy accorded it in Malay cultures. Cultural sanction for the behavior flows out of the importance of amok in the martial context, whether as an act of bravery in defense of the honor of one's leader or as an effective tactical maneuver in battle. Amok behavior is honorable. It is self-sacrificial behavior of the highest order, behavior that treads the fine line between heroism and insanity. The individual who dies committing martial amok dies an honorable death. Brandishing the weapons his people know, he sallies forth a greatly feared man, a courageous warrior. Ancient tales and ethical codes praise and reinforce his actions. Muslim belief and practice may to some extent further buttress his behavior.

When individuals outside the martial context engage in behavior similar in form to martial amok--what is here termed solitary amok--there is in the social reaction to the behavior a transference of at least some of the honor attaching in the martial realm. In life, exigencies sometimes arise that for some individuals demand to be addressed by amok behavior. To exhibit such behavior and encounter the attendant vast risk to life and limb means that an individual must, temporarily at least, go out of his mind, experience mata gelap, display total commitment. The transference of honor and respect from the martial context, the spectacular exhibition of supreme commitment in a manner inducing fear and awe in others, and the oft-times life and death finality of the solitary amok episode all combine to account for the element of respect and legitimacy accorded it by Malay peoples. What is common to most of the descriptions of behavior labeled amok is a constellation of symptoms, involving sudden, frenzied, generally indiscriminate homicidal behavior where bladed weapons are employed and where the amok-runner claims no memory of the episode. But the materials reviewed in this investigation indicate the existence of two separate etiological clusters in the genesis of amok behavior, one where the behavior is reactive and with motive, and one where it is wholly spontaneous and motiveless. Both must be considered in accounting for the existence and frequency of amok. Past etiological analyses have concentrated on one of these categories or on one or more factors associated with one of these categories and thus fall short of providing a comprehensive explanation of the phenomenon.

One exception to the pattern is the amok classification scheme developed by Gimlette in 1901 and extended by Fletcher in 1938.[35] Fletcher divides amok cases into two main classes: "(i) those occurring in persons suffering from some recognized pathological condition, such as manic-depressive insanity . . . or post-malarial psychosis; and (ii) those occurring in persons who are apparently sane and healthy."[36] The latter class of cases had already been divided by Gimlette into two categories, true and false amok.

In true amok the man kills without rhyme or reason, and there is complete amnesia afterwards. . . . The . . . characteristics of true amok [include]: (i) it is a sudden paroxysmal homicide, with evident loss of self-control; (ii) there is a prodromal period of mental depression; (iii) there is a fixed idea to persist in reckless homicide, without any motive; and (iv) there is subsequent loss of memory for the acts committed.

In false amok the man starts by avenging himself on an enemy and then works himself up into a rage to make a murderous attack on everyone within reach. In such cases there is some motive for the amok, and the loss of memory is absent or doubtful.[37]

The distinction noted by Gimlette was intended to instruct the colonial judiciary in Malaya regarding the appropriate disposition of amok cases, Gimlette believing insanity could be claimed rightfully in cases of "true" amok but not so in cases of "false" amok. Actually, the only valid distinction in the two types of amok delineated by Gimlette appears to rest on the presence or absence of motive. The other characteristic Gimlette specifies as distinguishing the two types, whether or not there was "loss of memory for the acts committed," was found in this investigation to be invariably present. The terms true amok and false amok are misleading, culpable and non-culpable or reactive-motivated and spontaneous-unmotivated amok representing more accurate designations.

However, the distinction between committing solitary amok with or without a motive is crucial in understanding the wide range of episodes included under the label amok. Amok behavior represents a traditional culture-specific symptom constellation capable of being either purposefully initiated or spontaneously and unintentionally manifested. In the former category--reactive-motivated amok--fall those cases of amok behavior that are reactions to a felt need to restore or avenge the loss of personal dignity suffered as a result of insult or misfortune (malu). In the second category--spontaneous-unmotivated amok--fall those cases which are an expression of this culturally conditioned symptom complex but which result from an organic disturbance.

Type I--Reactive-Motivated Solitary Amok

Wallace has stated that "it may be taken as axiomatic that it is the concern of all human beings to maintain an image of themselves as persons competent to attain their essential goals."[38] Awareness of incompetence in any sphere of life generates shame and anxiety. It is postulated here that the purposeful acts of solitary amok committed by apparently sane, healthy Malays were characterized by the common element of a felt sense of personal inadequacy or incompetence in the face of events that generated shame or a sense of futility. There was a desire to relieve the resultant anxiety through acts which restored dignity and self-respect. Gullick quotes a Malay proverb that is apropos: "In the last resort it is better to run amuck than to perish by inches; rather be eaten by a

crocodile than nibbled by small fish."[39] Whether
the cause of shame or futility was rooted in oppressive social structures, in personal insult, in
misfortune or bad luck, in a simple self-assessment
of personal inferiority, or in some combination of
these factors, some Malay males believed that the
appropriate response was an act of generalized
vengeance, a spectacular ultimate act demonstrating
prowess and commanding the fear-struck respect of
others. Just as with the martial amok-runners, the
high probability of suffering death in the course of
this act was no deterrent, for the likelihood of
just such a result was basic to the awe reserved for
the act and actor.

Some have speculated, and it seems plausible
that a generalized weariness of life and an explicit
desire for death may have intervened between the
overwhelming feeling of shame and the resolution to
run amok. This intervening period is the period of
sakit hati, the brooding that often, possibly
always, characterized the reactive-motivated
solitary amok episode. It was during this period
that resolve built to run amok, an act representing
for some Malays a means of escape from intolerable
feelings of shame or futility, an exit affording a
semblance of personal honor and merit. Thus the
solitary amok-runner was motivated by a desire to
escape from a life he believed did not afford him
personal dignity, the escape--death--to be accomplished in a manner that appeared to offer the only
means of mitigating the shame and hopelessness
pervading his consciousness. Whether he realized it
or not, he exited in a display of behavior with
origins in the acts of the traditionally revered
martial amok-runner.

As the act of amok was contemplated, the
prospect of being in front of one's fellows, an
object of collective pursuit, the frightful blood
and gore likely to be encountered, an uncertainty
about and lack of control over how events would
unfold, the near inevitability of being killed--all
combined with the excitement of the prospect of
imminent retributive vengeance and recapture of
personal dignity to form a psychological amalgam
that gradually built to frenzied eruption. The mind
was flooded, overwhelmed. The individual seized a
weapon, lashed out at the person nearest him, and
probably simultaneously experienced mata gelap;
finally, a potent physical force energized by the
psychology of frenzy unleashes a culturally
preprogrammed set of largely indiscriminate

homicidal acts against individuals in the environs. Ultimately the episode could end only with his capture, with completely disabling wounds, or--most likely--with his death. There could be no turning back, no reconsideration of the appropriateness of his actions.

To have been captured while engaged in amok in traditional Malay society most likely would have meant an intolerable, nearly irrevocable status of slavery or debt bondage or else--in those areas where non-Malay influences had penetrated--death by execution, death on the terms of someone else rather than on terms over which one has a degree of control. To be captured while engaged in amok in late nineteenth century Malaya or Indonesia would have meant execution or incarceration in a prison or lunatic asylum--all prospects far removed from the denouement sought by the amok-runner in wilfully initiating the episode. Indeed, on this point we will build our thesis that the colonial experience and response to amok were critical factors in its gradual decline.

Type II--Spontaneous Unmotivated Solitary Amok

A second category of solitary amok cases involves episodes that appear not to have been wilfully initiated. They were spontaneous, unmotivated manifestations of the amok syndrome that were by-products of organic disturbances, most likely the delirium or post-febrile mania sometimes accompanying certain infectious diseases, especially malaria. In these cases the individuals involved manifested a behavioral syndrome given form and content by the culture in which it was found, probably only one set of behaviors from a broad culturally-conditioned repertoire of responses potentially available for expression in such circumstances.[40] While probably infrequent, such individuals occasionally did exhibit the amok syndrome, thus constituting part of the universe of amok cases to be taken into account in analyzing the phenomenon.

While this investigation revealed no definite instances of amok behavior among the Malays of Malaysia and Indonesia being the intended or acci- dental result of hemp consumption, the aforemen- tioned analyses by Chevers and Dhunjibhoy are relatively convincing that such a link sometimes did exist in the Indian context. Such could also have been the case in Malaysia and Indonesia and might account for some spontaneous, unmotivated amok episodes. If so, the near total absence of any mention of hemp consumption in the many accounts of amok reviewed for the Malaysian context appears to indicate that, at most, it could have been of etiological significance in only a small proportion of the total number of amok episodes.

It is to be emphasized that an expression of non-purposeful, spontaneous amok accompanying severe psychological pathology as defined by Western classification schema is a notion for which this investigation has revealed no supporting evidence. In his typology, Fletcher implies that this occurs, but none of the cases of amok reviewed in the present study include information that would indicate severe pre-episode psychopathology. Rather it appears that only when amok accompanies the organic-based disturbances mentioned above is there any question about the prior sanity or health of the amok-runner.

Thus, the factor of most etiological significance in the genesis of spontaneous unmotivated solitary amok lies in physiological infection. Fitzgerald, Van Loon, and Galloway present evidence to indicate that amok behavior sometimes accompanied the fever-induced delirium of malaria or the post-febrile mania that sometimes follows malaria, dengue, and other fever-inducing infections. In these cases the display of amok behavior was spontaneous with no contemplative period of _sakit hati_.

Perhaps in his delirium the afflicted Malay envisioned himself under attack or under threat of possession by one or more of the maleficent spirits so numerous in the traditional Malay world, and, making use of the weaponry available in this environment, suddenly flailed out indiscriminately at individuals he saw as embodied manifestations of these evil forces. The behavior was culturally conditioned. Action such as this is what a Malay sometimes must do when confronted by a potent enemy.

In outward appearance the behavior exhibited in disease-induced spontaneous amok varied little if any from that displayed in wilful amok. Obviously the threatened observers of the episode had little interest in determining whether or not the amok behavior was initiated intentionally. Sooner or later the amok-runner was wounded but continued to attack or attempt to evade his pursuers until, finally, a victim of multiple wounds and blows, he succumbed. On occasion he would be stunned and secured or pinioned with the amok-catcher and subdued, but as we have seen, live capture of amok-runners apparently was not common. Like his counterpart who ran amok intentionally, the surviving individual whose amok behavior was engendered physiologically had no memory of the amok episode.

Summary

While the distinction between reactive-motivated and spontaneous-unmotivated solitary amok makes more intelligible the etiology of the pattern, it also aids in understanding the gradual decrease over time in the frequency with which the syndrome was exhibited. It is my contention that the changing social context in late nineteenth and early twentieth century Malaysia and Indonesia was marked by forces that altered significantly the social factors in traditional Malay society that generated amok behavior. The changes which occurred meant that by 1925 there was an almost total disappearance of reactive-motivated amok. It appears reasonable to conclude that by the twentieth century an increasing proportion of a decreasing number of amok episodes were of the spontaneous, unmotivated type with the occasional cases reported in the last sixty years probably almost solely of this latter type. The analysis now shifts to an explanation of these trends.

Chapter 6

SOLITARY AMOK: INCIDENCE AND SOCIAL CONTEXT

The British and Dutch colonial presence during
the last half of the nineteenth and early part of
the twentieth centuries presented forces that
engendered rapid and profound social change in
Malaya and Indonesia. While the Dutch presence in
Indonesia had been an important influence for
several hundred years, its impact heightened and
extended beyond Java to encompass the Archipelago
more pervasively during this period. Rapid tech-
nological advance in the West and the occurrence of
dramatic changes in the social structure of nineteenth century Europe fostered change in the
colonies, as well, at an unprecedented rate. An
increased need for Malaysian and Indonesian raw
materials and produce and a sense of a moral obliga-
tion to bring "enlightenment and progress" to the
non-Western world, combined to generate dramatic
alterations in indigenous social structures.[1]
Of foremost importance in the transformation
of traditional social organization was the establishment of political dominance by the British and
Dutch, a dominance based ultimately on superior
military force but achieved in large part, especially in Malaya, without extensive armed conflict.
Calculated formation of alliances with indigenous
forces, skillful conflict mediation, more ordered
and consistent judicial organization, and new,
expanded economic opportunities for the indigenous
populations were all critical factors in the general
pacification of societies traditionally marked by
considerable internal strife and frequently oppressive social institutions. However one may feel
about their ultimate cost-benefit ratio to the
indigenes, the cumulative effects altered a pre-
existing social context that had supported the
occurrence of amok, the result being a gradual
demise of the behavior.
The reader familiar with the histories of
Malaysia and Indonesia will find no new revelations

in the historical analysis to follow. For those not so familiar, such an overview is necessary, since it is the linkage hypothesized between these historical experiences and the amok phenomenon that is ultimately central to the study at hand.

The Traditional Social Context: Malay Political Organization

Gullick, in his important work, <u>Indigenous Political Systems of Western Malaya</u>, has probably most correctly and fairly described prevailing political organization in pre-colonial Malaya.[2] It is within the context described by Gullick that the pronounced strife and disorder to be discussed below were generated and sustained for several centuries for a substantial proportion of Malay peoples of the Peninsula and probably of the Archipelago generally.

Malay society was traditionally divided into two distinct social groups, a ruling class and a subject class, with distinctions based on birth and clearly demarcated by custom and belief. Territorially, peninsular Malaya comprised a number of independent states, each ruled over by an hereditary monarch known by the title <u>yang di-pertuan</u> (Malay), <u>raja</u> (Hindu), or <u>sultan</u> (Islamic). Within the state were a number of territorial chiefs, usually holding the areas in which they lived. At the next level came minor chiefs and village headmen who bore responsibility for administration, revenue collection, and generating manpower for war or joint labor projects. At the base of the social system was the peasant farmer, engaged for the most part in a subsistence agricultural economy usually based on wet or dry rice cultivation. Additionally, on both sides of the Peninsula, many made a living from fishing in sea or estuary.

The authority of the various rulers was circumscribed sharply by the extent to which they could control and command their territorial chiefs, with control often being achieved not at all or only in a very marginal fashion. Besides prestige, the rank of chief brought to the holder and his kin the right to "a share in the economic resources of the state in the form of taxation and toll, monopolies and concessions, produce, and labor or followers."[3] In general, while some exceptions must be made by time and place, the Malay political system was seldom characterized by any form of centralized authority. Roff declares that

In the absence of adequate communications or of any form of centralized administration, only a sultan possessing personal authority beyond the ordinary could expect to be, in effect, more than _primus inter pares_, a district chief among district chiefs. . . . Proportionate to their power, chiefs commonly retained a great deal more income than they surrendered and achieved positions closely rivaling that of their rulers. In this situation there was a strong ambivalence within the ruling class, marked by jealousies and tendencies toward strife and fission, which were counterbalanced, however, by a recognition of the values and virtues of the sultanate as a validating mechanism for the whole system. It was to the advantage of the chiefs to maintain the sultanate . . . as a basis for their position _vis-a-vis_ each other, as a source of prize in dynastic maneuvering, and as the embodiment of the larger political unit with its advantages for trade and defense.[4]

Roff's description of the retinue of the typical chief is instructive for understanding some of the problems generated by traditional Malay political organization.

The basis and emblem of authority was manpower, so that much depended on the ability of a chief to gather and retain a following from among his own kinsmen and from the peasants. A typical chief's household consisted of dependent kin performing the necessary tasks of administering his lands and acting as secretaries or accountants and tax gatherers; of mercenaries and free volunteers who provided a permanent, if often idle, armed force; and of debt-bondsmen and slaves who filled a great variety of service roles from household domestics and concubines for the chief and his followers to boatmen and gardeners. Though the district chief's household was not in absolute terms particularly large, it was sizable in relation to most Malay agricultural communities. Being almost entirely nonproductive, it relied heavily on the peasantry for its maintenance. To supplement the agricultural labor supplied by the chief's and his kinsmen's debt-bondsmen, use was made of the institution of kerah or corvée under which the inhabitants of all the villages in the district were obliged to contribute labor for working the fields, for collecting forest products, and for other public or private work from clearing paths to erecting buildings.[5]

Summarizing the effects of the structure of the upper echelons of the traditional Malay political organization, Gullick states as follows:

There was in effect a "spoils system" under which a fortunate minority in each state held office and could live on the revenues of their districts while a larger number of younger sons, dispossessed heirs and roaming adventurers obtained a precarious living as hangers-on or as free-lance Ishmaels whose hands were against every man. It was an unstable system since there were no absolute rules to determine the succession to a vacant office and there was every inducement to intrigue both within the same family and between rival families. The prizes were few, the competitors many, and the rules of the game . . . were often broken.[6]

At the lowest level of the ruling structure came the village headman, or penghulu, a figure of major importance in Malay village life. The headman served as the link between peasant and local chief and was usually rooted in the small community which he was charged with overseeing. The duties of the headman were many, "ranging from keeping the peace, arbitrating in disputes, and surrendering serious offenders to his chief, to tax collection, organization of kerah labor, and keeping the district chief generally informed about village affairs."[7]
The potential abuses of the political organization are summarized well by Roff.

114

The subordinate position of the ra'ayat [subject class] was held in question by neither side, nor was the right of members of the ruling class to receive on demand a wide range of goods and services in return for protection and the perpetuation of general welfare. The Malay peasant commonly held right to his land only in terms of occupation and use; though in practice this conferred reasonable security of tenure, these rights were revocable at will by chief or ruler. Accumulation of property, where it occurred, was prone to be visited by envious expropriation on the part of the raja, and indebtedness frequently led to the form of personal servitude known as debt-bondage. The system of kerah labor, while ensuring the maintenance of the ruling class and the upkeep of such communal facilities as village paths, landing stages and mosques, was often onerous and demanding.

Clearly, in a society such as this in which control over all aspects of life tended to be concentrated in the ruling class, privilege sanctioned by custom might easily be abused. It is not difficult to find instances of cruelty, oppression, and injustice.[8]

Prevailing Conditions in the
Peninsula and Archipelago

The state of indigenous social structures and processes as reported by most contemporary eighteenth and nineteenth century European observers is one rife with conflict, oppression and disordered government. Even allowing for a degree of self-serving exaggeration, these reports appear generally to have been accurate. Scores of such accounts exist but only a few will be cited here.

Raffles, writing in 1817 about the Peninsula and Archipelago generally, declares:

The causes which have tended most to the depression of the Malayan tribes . . . are the civil commotions to which every state is liable, from the radical want

115

of strength in the sovereign; the constant wars between petty chieftains and heads of villages; the ill-defined succession to the throne . . .; the prevalence of piracy in all the Eastern Seas; the system of domestic slavery, and all its concomitant evils, as wars for the purpose of procuring slaves, and the want of confidence between family and family, man and man; the want of a generally-established and recognized system of laws, civil and criminal; the want of a similar system of commercial regulations respecting port duties, anchorage, and other charges, to prevent arbitrary exactions and impositions in the various Malayan ports; and, finally, the monopoly of trade assumed by the Malayan rajas. . . . The prevalence of piracy on the Malayan coasts, and the light in which it was viewed as an honourable occupation, worthy of being followed by young princes and nobles, is an evil of ancient date, and intimately connected with the Malayan habits. The old Malayan romances, and the fragments of their traditional history, constantly refer with pride to piratical cruizes.[9]

Raffles' description is less applicable to Java where the Dutch influence had been much more pervasive than elsewhere in Indonesia. But in Java also a similar state of affairs was of recent memory. "Until within the last sixty years [roughly 1750-1810], when the Dutch first obtained a supremacy over the whole island, the provinces under the native administration had for several centuries been in a continual state of warfare."[10] While the "rude state of society" depicted by Raffles may not have characterized comparatively heavily settled Java so much as it did the rest of the Peninsula and Archipelago, nevertheless historically it had been present to some extent. The earlier, more intense Dutch presence in Java had simply meant a somewhat earlier beginning for the process of pacification and general societal transformation under the European aegis.

The Malay, Abdullah bin Abdul Kadir, vividly describes conditions in the 1830s in the Malaysian east coast states of Pahang, Trengganu, and

Kelantan. Writing of Trengganu, he says the following:

> [Everyone] carried four or five javelins and a kris and a cutlass. Their work consists of carrying weapons hither and thither. . . . All the evils which I have mentioned are due to the oppression of the Rajas and the badness of their rule. The common people are in a dilemma. Their point of view is that it is better to stay poor and avoid trouble, living from hand to mouth; for if a man does acquire property or a fine house or a planation or estate of any size, a Raja is sure to find some way or other to get hold of it; or he may demand a loan or a gift. And, if the man refuses, the Raja confiscates his property; if he resists, he and his whole family are killed; fines are also levied. So Trengganu remains thinly populated, and foreigners are afraid to live there, and there are no merchants.[11]

With respect to the prevalence of piracy, Miller states the following:

> Pirates had ranged from the Indian Ocean to the China Sea for centuries. The seas around the Indies and Borneo were the happy hunting-grounds of thousands of pirates, the Illanuns from the island of Mindanao, and the Balanini from Sulu. Around the Malay peninsula itself were Malay, Bugis and Achinese pirates. . . . The whole Malaysian region was particularly favourable for piracy because the innumerable estuaries, deep creeks, rivers and narrow channels were excellent hideaways either for an attack or for a quick escape. . . . Callous and cold blooded . . . [the pirates] impassively tortured and killed their captives or sent them into slavery. Thousands of men and women disappeared every year from villages after raids by pirates. They were sold as slaves to rulers, major chiefs and petty nobility in depots which existed in the extensive

archipelago for the sale of pirate loot,
both human and material. . . . The rigid
trading policies of the Dutch, which
destroyed the local inter-island trade,
turned rajas and chiefs to backing
pirates either openly or covertly in
order to replenish their depleted
treasures. The royal patrons provided
arms and gunpowder in return for a share
of the plunder and royal patronage made
[sic] piracy an "honourable" profession
in the archipelago. . . . By the 1820's
the situation was so bad that local
trade around the peninsula almost came
to a halt.[12]

With the discovery of extensive tin deposits
at Larut in Perak in the 1840s, there was engendered
another source of disorder in the Peninsula. Chinese
laborers poured into the area, and protracted warfare between two major Chinese factions ensued over
a twenty-five year period. According to Miller:

Stockades littered the region and tracks
between them were constantly under
ambush. By 1872 almost every Chinese
mining village in Larut had been burned
down and almost every mine had ceased to
operate. Clarke [Governor, Straits
Settlements] was to describe Larut as
"one huge cockpit where nothing but
fighting and murder and violence and
piracy" was going on.[13]

The dispute among the Chinese factions for
control of the tinfields spread to the seas as each
sought reinforcements. This served to resuscitate
piracy which by 1850 had been brought under a degree
of control around the Peninsula. In addition, the
Chinese troubles became interwoven with the
perennial Malay royal succession dispute in Perak,
where three branches of the royal family rotated in
providing the ruler, a system inevitably leading to
conflict and strife. Civil war broke out in Perak
in the 1850s as a result of problems surrounding
succession. Then in 1871 when the ruler, Sultan
Ali, died, strife was again renewed with the two
sides each enlisting one of the warring Chinese
factions to fight on its behalf--in exchange for
rights of exclusivity in the tinfields. Civil war
was again imminent.

Winstedt captures the plight of the Malay states with a collection of comments.

Civil war, tyranny and bad administration had taken the heart out of the peasant. Begbie has told how on the islands off Singapore all stimulus to industry was destroyed by the rapacity of the chiefs. . . . Newbold has noted how in the '30's of the 19th century the population of Muar was reduced to 2,400 "through the mis-government and apathy of the feudal sovreign; owing to which perpetual broils exist among the petty chiefs, causing insecurity of person and of property, and eventually driving out of the country all the cultivating and trading classes of the community. The honest peasant, in many instances, is compelled from sheer necessity to turn robber; and the coasts, instead of being crowded with fishermen, swarm with pirates. These remarks, indeed, may be extended to the whole of the Peninsula." Writing at the same period Munshi Abdullah [tells] of similar conditions in Trengganu. "Four or five fellows came and invited me to talk . . . [saying] they could no longer endure the tyranny of Malay rule. 'Every day,' they said, 'we have to work for the Raja at our own cost and without food being supplied to ourselves or our families. Our boats, crops and live-stock are liable to be seized by the Raja without payment. If the Raja wants our property or our daughters, we cannot withstand him. If we object, we are stabbed to death. Try to emigrate and we are killed, if caught, and our property is confiscated.'" Even the Malay system of taxation encouraged reckless improvidence and discouraged thrift and enterprise. Cockfighting won the chiefs popularity and filled their coffers. In Kedah there was a tax on every plough, in Pahang on coconut oil.[14]

A final graphic description of the oppressiveness of political organization in Pahang at the time of British intervention comes from Hugh Clifford.

The case of the amok of Meng reported in chapter three might be recalled here. Miller summarizes Clifford's comments on Pahang thus:

> The four major chiefs had the power of life and death over all the people residing in their respective territories. The Sultan had a bodyguard known as the Budak Raja (King's Youths), drawn from the nobility; they dressed magnificently in brilliant coloured silks, were armed with dagger, sword and spear, and passed most of their time in 'making love and in playing games of chance.' They guarded the ruler on his walks, they rowed his boat, hunted game with him and snared turtle-doves for him, carried his messages, levied fines on his behalf (and theirs), killed those who offended him (and them), seized property which he (or they) wanted, and abducted women for his household (or theirs). They represented the only force by which the State . . . was policed. The average peasant possessed no rights, and, . . . 'he and his were always and completely at the mercy of those of their neighbours who were more powerful than themselves.' But then, 'the Malays, in common with other more civilized folk, had worked out for themselves unaided a theory of government on feudal lines which bears a starling resemblance to the European models of a long-passed epoch. But there they had halted. To live in independent Malaya is to live in the Europe of the thirteenth century.'[15]

Ruling class exactions combined with the lack of an overarching source of authority in traditional Malay political organization share responsibility for the existence of the seemingly ubiquitous civil strife and oppressiveness characterizing life for so long in so much of the Peninsula. While, in Gullick's words, "In the first half of the nineteenth century there had been a rough and ready political equilibrium between robber barons,"[16] there simply was no indigenous source with the capability and will to institute and enforce a comprehensive, widespread system of law and order.

Thus, there existed very ample opportunity to engage in lawlessness, warfare, oppression, and general rapacity and, as we have seen, no lack of opportunists.

British Intervention and Ascendance in the Peninsula

It was against this backdrop that direct British intervention occurred in Malaya in 1874. The Dutch, as they extended and made more pervasive their influence in the outer islands, frequently encountered similar conditions. But with British intervention and the extension of Dutch influence, this context changed dramatically as the modernizing forces of late nineteenth century colonialist imperialism began to influence the operation of traditional Malay social structures and processes. The social context within which martial and solitary amok had been generated and sustained was altered, with one result being a near disappearance of martial and reactive-motivated amok.

The character and details of the British intervention and early colonial period in Malaya are well-documented and have been the subject of extensive analyses.[17] An exhaustive review of this period is not integral to the present analysis; however, a brief chronology and a description of several key features of the British presence are necessary.

During the period of 1824 to 1914 the whole of Malaya came by stages under British administration. The original base of British rule was the Straits Settlements formed in 1826 by the merger of Singapore, Penang, and Malacca and administered as a dependency of the Government of India. To safeguard these ports, the British established a sphere of influence in the Peninsula, negotiating a settlement with Siam (Thailand) in 1826 which fixed the limits of Siamese control at the southern boundaries of Kedah, Perlis, Kelantan, and Trengganu and left the British viewing all Malaya from Perak and Pahang southwards as being within this sphere. Until the 1860s British interest in the Malay states lay primarily in trying to prevent wars and exclude foreign interference. By the mid-nineteenth century the British and their commercial interests were firmly entrenched in the Straits Settlements. Suffering setbacks in trade in the 1850s and 1860s, the Straits merchants began to look for opportunities to develop new interests in the Peninsula in order to offset their losses. However the disorder and strife in the Peninsula endangered existing investments and impeded expansion of trade. Commercial pressures on the Straits Government to correct the situation thus became one of the reasons propelling the British into direct intervention.

With the 1867 transfer of the Straits Settlements from the Government of India to a Crown Colony directly under the control of the Colonial Office in London, a worsening situation in the Peninsula, and a British fear of German or other foreign intervention, the stage was set for direct action. The appointment of Sir Andrew Clarke as Governor in 1873 was the beginning of the Residential system of British administration in the Malay States.

In 1874 came the appointment of the first British Residents in the Malay States, appointments made at the behest of the indigenous rulers. In this year, Residents were accepted by Perak, Selangor, and one of the Negri Sembilan, Sungai Ujong. By 1888 they had been accepted also in the whole of Negri Sembilan and in Pahang. From this foothold the British initiated pursuit of what, at least for the officials in the field, were dual objectives. First, the British sought to create political stability, ordered government, and a general tranquility so as to enable rapid economic and commercial development of Malaya's natural resources. Probably secondary, but serving as a moral rationale for the colonial enterprise, was an expressed concern for the welfare and advancement of the Malay people.

Nominally serving only as "advisers" and attempting to maintain traditional structures and processes as well as to secure the participation and cooperation of the traditional ruling elite, the residents pursued conciliation of the ruling class. In centralizing authority within each state and eroding the independent authority of the district chiefs, they allowed the sultans to assume real as well as ritual authority. The sultans were consulted on matters affecting the state as a whole and served as advisors on Malay matters. With privy purse and handsome personal allowances and pensions financed out of the increasing wealth of the country, the rulers fared well. The remainder of the Malay aristocracy was provided with incomes commensurate with prior rank and allowed to participate in some of the tasks of administration. With the British assuming responsibility for directing administrative and judicial functions and enacting laws prohibiting exactions from the peasantry, the district chiefs lost their means of support; therefore, to compensate the chiefs, a system of pensions and allowances was established which provided for them a relatively comfortable security and allowed them to maintain differences of status and rank. The various segments of the traditional ruling class found little with which to quarrel in a system constructed so skillfully and implemented so tactfully.

State Councils were formed in the four protected states which dealt with a wide range of governmental business and which provided the appearance that independent Malay initiative was being preserved. The work of the Councils embraced everything

> from mining leases, tariff regulation, taxation, and public works to the appointment and jurisdiction of penghulus and the consideration of Muslim personal law. They decided claims for allowances and pensions to chiefs and dependent kin, legislated for the abolition of debt-bondage, and discussed the scales for the first railway charges.[18]

Despite appearances, it was the British Residents, backed by the final authority of the governor of the Straits Settlements, who exercised direct control over every aspect of government--revenue collection and disbursement, customs and other dues, lands and mines, police, and courts. Roff summarizes the situation by stating that the assistance the Malay members of the Councils

> gave to the Resident in the early years of the system--in providing a touchstone of public feeling and in transmitting his authority--was of the greatest importance in the transition to British rule, but it was an assistance that by its very nature gave Malays less and less of a real share in the determination of public policy as the complexity of government grew.[19]

The lowest level of the traditional ruling structure, the penghulus or headmen, were of prime importance in the establishment of British rule;

more than anyone else they carried British administration to the villages. Roff describes succinctly their duties and importance.

> They received a moderate salary and were given administrative charge, under the European officer responsible for the district as a whole, of a subdivision called a mukim. . . . Their principal duties were to keep the peace in the villages of their mukim; to try, and fine, petty offenders; to report on the general progress of the mukim; and to enforce government regulations. With the passage of time, and of additional legislation concerning lands and crops, revenue, health, schooling, and much else, the tasks of the penghulu increased enormously in extent, though not in general character, so that he became the hardest worked and, in relation to his responsibilities, the poorest paid of all government officials. The British had good cause for gratitude and often expressed it.[20]

The introduction of British administration rapidly brought order and prosperity to the protected states. Perhaps the greatest innovation was the introduction of courts of justice presided over by European magistrates, frequently assisted by Malay magistrates. The penal code of the Straits Settlements was adapted from the Indian penal code, and the codes of criminal and civil procedure followed Indian and other British colonial patterns. Gradually, police duties were given to headmen and the police force overall reduced, signifying a policy of cooperation rather than intimidation. According to Winstedt:

> Under Malay rule . . . not even the justice of the central authority was fixed and unalterable, but it would vary according to the age and disposition of the Sultan and the suppleness of his advisers. One reign and even one district would see the mild old-world indigenous system of compensation in force; while a new ruler or a neighbouring chief would prefer some harsh provision of Hindu or Muslim law. Under the

British, justice, though often harsh, became everywhere uniform and always honest.[21]

In 1884 debt-slavery was abolished in Perak with some three thousand individuals set free. Selangor had already taken the lead in ending debt-slavery and in a short period of time every state in the Peninsula had followed suit.

Malay agriculture expanded rapidly following introduction of a system of land tenure based on the Torrens system of registered title brought to Malaya in the 1880s from South Australia.[22] Under this system, all land rights were vested in the sultan until granted in his name to a landholder. Titles granted in this manner were then entered in registers maintained by the government, and each landholder was given a copy of his registered title.

During the first twenty years of British control (1874-1894) comprehensive administrative structures were created to conduct the business of government in the protected states. They nearly always functioned in a highly efficient, orderly fashion. British administration made possible an unprecedented prosperity as revenues, services, and population grew simultaneously. During this period revenues flowed largely from tin mining, an enterprise that prospered mightily. Efficient tax collection and land administration measures were introduced; roads and railways were constructed; streams and rivers were cleared; education and public health facilities were provided. Perak's population grew from an estimated 80,000 in 1879 to 214,254 in 1891, and the population of the protected states trebled between 1874 and 1890.

During the 1890s it became clear to the British that a single Malay state was too small a unit for fully efficient management, and a major effort to centralize the government was initiated with the formation in 1895 of the Federated Malay States, consisting of Perak, Selangor, Negri Sembilan, and Pahang. It was argued that the four protected states were drifting apart in matters of justice, taxation, and land settlement and that administrative uniformity demanded the centralized power of the Federation with its chief executive, the resident-general. After persuading the indigenous rulers to accept the plan, Frank Swettenham became the first resident-general in 1896.

Formation of the Federation eroded the

political power reserved for Malay rulers under the Residential system. Gullick notes that

> as the government machine grew larger its sheer size and complexity detached it from the Malay Sultans and it lost its Anglo-Malay quality as it responded to the needs of an expanding economy. . . . The transfer of power from the States to the new federal executive of the F. M. S. deprived the State Councils of their usefulness and vitality. After 1895 they had merely to rubber-stamp proposals handed down to them from a federal secretariat, remote and unapproachable.[23]

While the matters of excessive centralization and meaningful indigenous political participation were to be the foci of considerable controversy for the remainder of the British dominance in Malaya, there was little argument about the efficiency and prosperity brought by British administration. Numerous facts and figures are cited by various writers as indices of development, including this compilation by Hall:

> The population of the four states rose from 424,218 in 1891 to 678,595 in 1901. The revenue increased from just under 8½ million dollars in 1895 to just under 24 million dollars in 1905 and there was an appreciable surplus of revenue over expenditure. In 1874 the states did not boast of a single post office. In 1904 their postal services dealt with 10 million covers, issued money orders for more than 1½ million dollars, had in their savings banks deposits of 275,000 dollars, and maintained over 2,000 miles of telegraph wires. There were hospitals treating many thousands of patients and schools attended by 13,000 children. There were over 2,400 miles of good roads and 340 miles of railway built out of current revenue.[24]

With the 1909 Anglo-Siamese Treaty, the four northern Siamese-controlled Malay states of Kedah, Perlis, Kelantan, and Trengganu were brought under British control but, as the Unfederated Malay States

(UMS), they retained considerably greater autonomy than states of the Federation. They were soon joined in the UMS by Johore. British power was confined to the right to advise and, in general, the unfederated states were characterized by Malay regimes tempered by British influence rather than by British control. In the UMS the British did not confront the anarchy and disorder that had preceded their arrival into the FMS in 1874. "Accordingly," Gullick declares, "the British Advisers had no opportunity or occasion to assume all-pervasive executive control and the very slow tempo of economic progress [in the four northern states] precluded the development of a new and alien bureaucratic machine."[25] However, while the influence had been less direct than in the FMS, these states also had been affected over the preceding forty years by the advent of the pax Britannica in the Peninsula.

With the production of rubber joining the mining of tin as a major industry, Malaya experienced a profound economic revolution which during the first twenty years of the twentieth century brought the country into the forefront of world commercial development. With development came problems and conditions with which indigenous Malay leaders were ill-equipped to cope. "Malaria control, agricultural chemistry, modern educational policy, the world price of tin and rubber . . . became the main concerns of the government, and they could no longer be dealt with by the old method of a Resident using his persuasive powers upon sultans and chiefs."[26] Gullick notes that in some degree there developed two economic systems side by side:

> the peasant economy of the Malay villages and the "export economy" of the rubber, tin, and other major industries. However, the Malay peasant was drawn into the export or cash economy inasmuch as he became accustomed to earn a money income with which to purchase some of his requirements and for this purpose sold his rubber, surplus rice, copra, etc. as the case might be.[27]

The social context and forces that had spawned and maintained the occurrence of solitary amok had been deeply and irrevocably transformed in a very short period of time. Roff summarizes well the changes of the traditional context.

The establishment of internal peace and
ordered government removed the constant
fear of embroilment in the rivalries of
Malay aristocratic or Chinese mining
factions. The emasculation of the power
of the chiefs to require and exact
tribute and service no doubt lightened
the burden of toil; debt-bondage was
eradicated; and the introduction of a
system of law based neither on power nor
on social status but on the rights of
the individual removed many of the
uncertainties of life from both wrong-
doer and wronged. Though the Malay
gained little from the vast public
expenditure of the states in the latter
part of the century, he was equally
asked to contribute little. The annual
quitrent he was now required to pay on
his land in recognition of occupancy and
use was a small price to pay for the
indefeasible title obtainable after the
introduction of the first effective land
legislation in the 1890s.[28]

Late Nineteenth and Early Twentieth Century Dutch Impact in Indonesia

Meanwhile in the Indonesian Archipelago, where
the details of European intervention differed
considerably from those of Malaya, changes similar
to those occurring in the Peninsula were being
generated. The history of Dutch dominance in
Indonesia is very long and complex, and detailed
consideration of this history is beyond the scope of
the present investigation. The historical factor of
most importance for present purposes is the
expansion of the Dutch. During the middle third of
the nineteenth century, Java was strongly affected
by the imposition of the Dutch-operated Cultivation
System, but it was not until late in the century
that the Dutch made economic and political inroads
into the rest of the Archipelago.[29]

The conditions of disorder and conflict
described earlier pervaded much of the Archipelago
for the greater part of the nineteenth century.
Warfare, slave trading, and piracy abounded.
However with the 1860s and 1870s came changes in
Dutch policy and in world economic forces that would
lead eventually to dramatic change in these
conditions.

In the Netherlands the economic oppression of
the Culture System and its vision of the Indies as a
business concern operating for the sole purpose of
providing profits for the mother country was
challenged successfully by the laissez-faire Liberal
element eventuating in the initiation of the so-
called Liberal Era in 1870, to last through 1900.
Hall notes that the Liberals "had two largely
contradictory objects--to free the native from
oppression and to make the Indies safe for the
individual capitalist."[30] A great period of private
enterprise ensued with vastly increased freedom and
security for individual investment. Control over
cultivation passed from the hands of government
officials to private contractors. The Agrarian Law
of 1870, besides providing legislation which would
prevent large amounts of land from being alienated
from Indonesian ownership, opened the way for a
major expansion of plantation agriculture, not only
in Java but in the outer islands as well, especially
Sumatra.

The capitalistic economic expansionism of the
last quarter of the century, Dutch fears of other
European powers, and the needs of Dutch industry for
raw materials combined to dictate assertion of
effective Dutch control in the outer islands.
Vlekke states that Liberal principles and policy

> would not permit leaving the outer
> islands to take care of themselves
> with all the consequences bound to
> follow . . .: piracy, disorder, local
> wars, and the consequent hampering of
> commerce, especially of Indonesian
> shipping. The new principles demanded
> that 'order and peace' should be secured
> all over the Archipelago, that head-
> hunting, and tribal feuds fought by
> order of petty warlords, should come to
> an end.[31]

Where resistance was encountered as the Dutch pushed
forward, military action ensued, with the result
being a number of minor campaigns, and a protracted
war against Aceh in northern Sumatra. Indigenous
rulers were required to sign the "Dorte Verklaring"
(Short Statement) empowering the colonial administration to issue directives regarding their exercise
of authority. Vlekke reports that "More than two
hundred and fifty potentates, some of whom were
rulers of large territories, while others were

merely local village or district chiefs, signed such a statement by which they became wholly subordinated to the authority of Batavia."[32]

By 1909, Dutch authority was established over nearly all of what would become the Republic of Indonesia. Existing rulers generally were allowed to retain their positions and some internal governmental functions, and selected Indonesian representatives were relied upon to handle day-to-day relations with the indigenous peoples; however, a far-ranging European civil service was given wide powers, not only supervisory but also of direct administration in numerous areas such as road and dam building, forestry, mining, and the control of village budgets.

As with British Malaya, the extension of Dutch rule to the outer territories brought with it numerous accouterments of modernization. A great amount of survey and development work occurred. Roads, dams, irrigation works, railways, telegraph and telephone networks, postal services, and harbor and dock facilities were developed in many areas, efforts that were to be further emphasized in the twentieth century with the advent of the "Ethical Policy." These developments were but physical indicators of the dramatic, rapid and pervasive social change that was taking place in Indonesia. As Tarling describes it, the expansion of Dutch administration generated "profound effects upon the traditional structure of society, undermining the old adat chiefs and old economic-political structures by new administrative and judicial structures, new tax requirements, new police and education measures."[33]

Several economic depressions near the close of the nineteenth century had a heavy impact on the economy of the Netherlands Indies and prompted attempts to correct the undesirable effects of the period of relatively unbridled laissez-faire economic liberalism.[34] The expectations of the Liberals that their polices would generate maximum benefit for both private entrepreneur and the general populace had gone unrealized. Private enterprise generated phenomenal achievements, but the benefits accrued primarily to the promoters, not to the laborers. From 1890 forward, the voices of humanitarian liberalism in the Netherlands stirred widespread indignation over an officially admitted trend of declining Indonesian welfare, and at the beginning of the twentieth century came adoption of the principle that Indonesia should be governed not for the benefit of the Netherlands, but for the benefit of the indigenous population. This "Ethical Policy" dictated a direct and active role for government in providing a variety of economic services, welfare programs, and schools.

With the Ethical Policy came even more intensive exploration and surveying, railway and road building, and expansion of shipping service and facilities. Substantial efforts were directed toward forest conservation, soil development, veterinary improvement, and expansion of agricultural and fisheries production. Irrigation works were further developed, and public health work was carried out on a larger scale. Additionally, the government began to establish village schools in much larger numbers and relaxed somewhat the restrictions on Indonesian enrollment in Dutch schools.

New investment capital came into the colony from British, American, and Dutch sources, all anxious to capitalize on an increasing world demand for tropical products. While much of this capital went into the traditional Java-grown crops of sugar, coffee, and tea, even more was invested in the products of the outer islands: tobacco, rubber, tin, and oil. Outside Java, estate agriculture and mining developed rapidly. Of foremost importance was the generation in the outer islands of a class of export-oriented Indonesian small holders and petty capitalists, signifying a significant expansion of Indonesian entrepreneurship which, when combined with a slowly increasing number of Western educated Indonesians, provided the basis for lessened Indonesian passivity.

By 1910, the pax Neerlandica extended throughout the Archipelago, innumerable political and social entities had become unified politically, and the indigenous populations of the outer islands were beginning to experience the effects of incipient modernization. Economic development had been tremendous, and colonial policy now dictated that a substantial share of the economic gain be plowed back into Indonesian society in the form of increased welfare services and benefits for the Indonesians. To implement and sustain a system with these objectives, the Dutch developed a modern administrative bureaucracy. Efforts at administrative decentralization in the direction of increased local and village autonomy were a noticeable failure.[35] The failure here parallels that experienced by the British in Malaya in the early 1900s in attempting to maintain meaningful Malay participation in government. In this respect, Bastin and Benda have concluded as follows:

> The demands of the modern colonial state, based on efficient territorial administration and on an increasing proliferation of technical and welfare services, simply could not be met by native institutions, whether at the level of Southeast Asian monarchy or at that of local and village government.[36]

While the objectives of the Ethical Policy fell far short of being realized during the period in which this policy was operative, it was during this time especially that the indigenous Indonesian population was forced to come to grips with modernization and the world economy--to develop a version of modernity adapted to the Indonesian context.[37] Steinberg, et al. state the problem well:

> The Indies of the early twentieth century incorporated a whole world of indigenous societies: large and small; Islamic, Hindu-Buddhist, Christian, and pagan; wet-rice growers, swidden cultivators, and traders; kingdoms and kin-groups; literate and nonliterate. There were certain commonalities in the historical experience, artistic traditions, and religious assumptions of those societies. But each had its own integrity, a distinct cultural tradition defined and enforced by its own language and shared by aristocrats and commoners alike. Members of those societies, as they sought to come to terms with modernity, had models to use, but they were foreign and difficult to translate. There were no pre-existing versions of modernity for any of the indigenous societies of the Indies, let alone for all of them in common. This was something that members of those societies had to do for themselves, if they chose to, an immense job of creating and recreating their identities. In a population that counted 40 million in 1905 and was divided into dozens of

distinct societies, the range of choices offered and paths of change to be followed were innumerable.[38]

The European Impact and Solitary Amok

Both in Malaya and Indonesia, the European effort to develop and protect diplomatic and economic interests, as well as efforts to bring the supposed benefits of modernization and progress to the indigenous populations, led to the introduction of a modern economic and administrative order, supported by a combination of administrative, police, and military power. Throughout the Peninsula and the Archipelago endemic conflict and disorder had been interdicted, while internal and external security were established. Probably for the first time in history, overarching governmental authorities as well as a degree of economic stability existed in both regions. 'Concurrent with these developments came a decreased occurrence of reactive-motivated solitary amok.

Because of the reduction in warfare among indigenous groups and the gradual elimination of piracy, behaviors and practices valued in martial contexts became less significant. The extent to which martial amok was still practiced in the nineteenth century is unclear; however, it is likely that as pacification became widespread there were fewer opportunities to use this tactic. In any event, the increased availability of firearms and modern weapons probably decreased the utility of martial amok considerably. And as marital amok became obsolete, the basis upon which reactive-motivated solitary amok acquired its cultural legitimacy was eroded.

For most Malays, especially in the Peninsula and the outer islands, European dominance relieved other oppressive aspects of the traditional social context. Slavery, debt bondage, forced tribute, and forced service were decreased or eliminated; property rights were established; and the power of chiefs and other authorities to act arbitrarily was curbed.

While the direct impact was less pervasive for Malays than for other resident ethnic groups, the profound changes in economic organization in both Malaya and Indonesia were still of major significance in the cultural transformation that began to take place in Malay society during this period. With economic change Malays were provided opportunities to participate in a cash economy where reward and status were increasingly determined by universalistic criteria involving individual effort and achievement. Although direct participation by Malays in the cash-based export economy was halting and far from universal, the economic forces involved fundamentally altered traditional Malay society. For one thing, political institutions were established by the colonial powers which provided continuous and relatively stable government able to guarantee individual rights and the legal framework necessary for the operation of the new economic order.

Legal systems based on the rights of the individual rather than on power and status meant the removal of "many of the uncertainties of life for both wrong-doer and wronged."[39] Whether in the framework of <u>adat</u> or European law or an amalgam of the two, more explicit and uniform guides for social action were established. Thus, improvements in the administration of justice created viable institutionalized alternatives both to passivity and to the assertion of force and coercion. Orderly pursuit of vengeance became the domain of a government possessing authority and operating effectively. Significantly diminished was the quasi-legitimacy previously adhering to the unregulated pursuit of vengeance and redress by the isolated individual. Not only did a regular system of law more explicitly identify such behavior as undesirable, no longer necessary, and outside the law, it also served to reduce the frequency of the behavior by making unlawful traditional practices which had sometimes driven men to run amok.

The Europeans also brought views about mental disorder and criminal behavior which differed from those traditionally held by the Malays. With the concrete manifestations of these beliefs--lunatic asylums, jails and prisons--came opportunities for a European judicial response other than execution of surviving amok-runners. The widely varying disposition of the cases of surviving amok-runners is reflective not only of ambivalence but also of an implicit European recognition of a need to differentiate among amok cases. Apparently assessments of culpability were sometimes based on distinctions at least roughly similar to the one drawn in this study between reactive-motivated and spontaneous, unmotivated solitary amok. Generally, the expanded range of judicial dispositions available to the Europeans was accompanied by an increased emphasis on trying to capture the amok-runner alive. Probably operating on the assumption that incarceration in an asylum or prison reflected a more humane, constructive orientation toward dealing with the solitary amok-runner, the Europeans were making more uncertain attainment of the amok-runner's objective of death by means of an act marked to some extent by residues of a culturally-defined meaning of heroic vengeance. Thus, at the same time that forces from the traditional context which might engender the motivation to run amok were lessening, amok was becoming a form of behavior less likely to accomplish the objective sought by the individual determined to assert his competence and dignity.

Elsewhere, Malay participation in or on the periphery of the newly-established cash economy meant an increasing emphasis on economic rationalism with the development of new attitudes and aptitudes, such as literacy and technical skills, which were required by the new system. Education became the most likely means of acquiring the necessary skills, habits, and attitudes. Among Malays education gradually began to displace birthright and forceful usurpation as the basis for successful functioning in the system. From the turn of the century forward, the provision of increased, if still woefully limited, opportunities for Malays to acquire formal education became a vital force in the transformation of traditional Malay society.

The forces of modernization also generated changes in the Malay personality. With the emphasis on economic rationalism and a stable government, new levels of individual autonomy became possible. More than ever before, the fate and destiny of the individual Malay lay with himself. The perspective of the individual Malay could begin to shift from the narrow confines of the traditional village or residential grouping to the more flexible and autonomous social relationships of the modern village or urban center, thereby avoiding or escaping the pressures of traditional structures in ways that were more effective than the traditional pattern of geographic mobility.

Certainly the advent of Western dominance in Malaya and Indonesia was accompanied by new inequities and sources of oppression and frustration for indigenous groups. These new stresses included the need to become involved in capitalist economies, altered avenues of political participation and decision-making which were less advantageous for some than had been traditional structures, necessarily deferential behavior toward the all-too-frequently self-righteous condescension of Westerners, and required participation in an administrative bureaucracy which, if protective of the general order, generated the frustrations frequently associated with such structures. Could not this complex of factors serve as a functional equivalent for the traditional strains and pressures and, like them, generate solitary amok by aggrieved and insulted individuals? A clear answer is difficult, but it seems probable that as Western control and its new set of pressures became pervasive, solitary amok simply lost its meaning as a symbolic gesture. The Westerner had brought rules and a social order so different and potent that traditional behaviors were called into question, by Malays as well as Westerners. As we have seen, the Westerner responded to solitary amok in ways that served to shear it of its symbolic significance.

In sum, during the period of 1875 to 1925 the social environment of Malay peoples in most of Malaya and Indonesia underwent fundamental and pervasive change. With the contextual changes outlined above, the factors generating reactive-motivated solitary amok were ameliorated, transformed, or altered so as to make this form of behavior obsolete as a meaningful, culturally sanctioned expression. The quasi-legitimacy that characterized solitary amok had begun to disappear into a remote past. The behavior pattern became increasingly a cultural memory of waning salience and acceptability.

The decreasing rate of occurrence of reactive-motivated solitary amok took place over a long period of time, undoubtedly far longer than that detailed in this investigation. A few cases continued to occur into the twentieth century. But by this time manifestations of amok behavior were predominantly of the spontaneous, unmotivated type with a physiological genesis, usually manifested during the states of delirium accompanying malaria or other fever-inducing infections. Although amok behavior was declining in significance, awareness and knowledge of the pattern remained. The continuing awareness was of sufficient strength to assure that the outward characteristics of amok would continue to represent for at least a while longer one set of culturally-conditioned behaviors available to and sometimes employed by the Malay experiencing delirium. If an individual predisposed to such behavior became delirious, happened to come by one of the many cutting weapons and instruments available even to the present day in the Malay world, took flight and initiated attacks upon those he perceived of as persecutors or foes, then there was nothing of an observable nature to distinguish his actions from those of the individual wilfully running amok.

With the advent of the medical and public health advancements of the twentieth century, malaria and the other amok-related delirium producing diseases came under a measure of control, particularly during the latter years of the first quarter of the century. With new knowledge, hospitals and medication, conditions which previously had led to situations where an individual might experience delirium became less common. Where they did occur, the individual experiencing delirium was more likely to be in an environment where his actions could be controlled.

Thus, certain of the conditions and forces responsible for spontaneous, unmotivated amok continued into the twentieth century while those generating the reactive-motivated amok pattern had disappeared or diminished in a far greater degree. With further inroads after 1925 in controlling the physiological bases for amok behavior and an ever-increasing temporal and psychological distance from the traditional Malay social context, a time was approaching when solitary amok in any form in the Malay world would be only a memory.

Chapter 7

SUMMARY

Summary of Findings

The Malay word amok, when used in the context
of human behavior, refers to frenzied, indiscriminate, homicidal aggression. Although most analyses
address only non-martial manifestations of this
behavior, what this study terms solitary amok, amok
has probably been more prominent historically within
the martial context. In both the Malay-inhabited
areas of Southeast Asia and in southern India, an
area with close ties to the Malay world, amok
behavior was an important battle tactic demanding
ultimate self-sacrifice, and it was therefore valued
and honored. Additionally in the Malay context but
not in the south Indian, there are repeated references to solitary, individualized amok occurring
outside the martial realm, both contemporaneous with
martial amok and after martial amok had ceased to be
a useful battle tactic. It is likely that amok
behavior in the martial realm fostered and rein-
forced the occurrence of such behavior outside the
martial context, with the curious quasi-legitimacy
accorded solitary amok by the Malays accruing
residually from the honor and legitimacy accorded
martial manifestations.

Because the best data on solitary amok comes
from the years 1800-1925 and because 1925 seems to
be the time when the behavior had virtually ceased,
this study reports on the characteristics and frequency of solitary amok episodes during these years.
It was found that the amok-runner was nearly always
a Malay male, twenty to forty years of age, and
usually a transient, temporarily resident in a
relatively heavily-populated area. With respect to
residence, however, no firm conclusions can be drawn
due to probable reporting biases.

Manifestations of solitary amok were never
anticipated in advance. Some episodes erupted
seemingly wholly spontaneously whereas other

139

episodes were preceded by a period of sullen brooding known as _sakit_ _hati_. The initial stages of the attack phase of the episode were often marked by apparently selective homicidal aggression against relatives or prior acquaintances, after which indiscriminate aggression occurred. Bladed, cutting weapons were employed almost universally in amok attacks because of availability, practical utility, and cultural desirability. Invariably present in surviving amok-runners was _mata_ _gelap_, total amnesia with respect to the attack phase of the episode.

The sustained ferocity of the amok attack meant that the most common response to solitary amok by Malays, Dutch, and British alike necessarily was to kill the amok-runner during the course of the attack. Several customary Malay practices would have encouraged restraint and live capture of the amok-runner, and the result of being captured generally would have been far different from the heroic death envisioned by many amok-runners, especially those who intentionally initiated amok episodes. To achieve his object, therefore, the amok-runner had to fight to the finish, sustaining his furious aggression to a point where his pursuers had no alternative but to slay him.

In the hope of deterring such episodes, the Dutch and British initially executed captured amok-runners. Toward the end of the nineteenth century, a response of incarceration in prisons or custodial insane asylums was employed at least as frequently as execution, the Europeans manifesting a decided ambivalence in dealing with solitary amok.

While the record is not conclusive, some evidence was found to support the assertion made frequently in the nineteenth century that the frequency of solitary amok had declined substantially over time. The widespread existence in Malay communities of a device the central purpose of which was to restrain amok-runners indicates strongly that solitary amok had been rather frequent and widespread geographically, and that it had existed over a long period of time.

Past observers have attributed amok to a variety of causes including drug intoxication, Muslim beliefs and practices, and physical illness. While neither drugs nor Islam were really significant causes, it is indeed true that malarial and other fever-inducing infections were linked to some amok episodes. The materials reviewed in this investigation suggested the existence of two

140

separate etiological clusters in the genesis of amok behavior.

Reactive-motivated amok was at least somewhat intentional and occurred in the face of shame or a sense of futility. To be killed while engaged in a spectacular act of generalized vengeance seems to have been viewed as a means of restoring or establishing dignity and self-respect. On the other hand, spontaneous, unmotivated amok was the result of organic disturbances and was not initiated wilfully. Rather, this second type of amok represents a culturally-conditioned symptomalogical syndrome manifested by people experiencing delirium. In such cases the contemplative period of _sakit_ _hati_ was absent.

The changing context of late nineteenth and early twentieth century British Malaya and the Netherlands East Indies was marked by forces that, in their cumulative effect, altered significantly traditional Malay society with the result that expressions of solitary amok virtually disappeared. Chief among these changes were the following: the establishment of peace and political stability in lands where conflict and disorder had dominated; economic development with an accompanying emphasis on economically rational behavior; the development of complex administrative structures enabling the business of government to be carried out effectively and pervasively; elimination of several traditional practices including debt-bondage, slavery, and arbitrary usurpation of land; and the development of a judicial system admitting of greater order and consistency in ensuring the rights of the individual. The factors that generated solitary amok were thus ameliorated, transformed, or altered so as to make this form of behavior obsolete as a meaningful, culturally sanctioned expression. Those cases of solitary amok which did take place in the twentieth century, especially after 1925, were probably predominantly of the spontaneous, unmotivated type with physiological causes. With further penetration of modernizing influences, with increasing control over the physiological bases for amok behavior, and with increasing temporal and psychological distance from the traditional Malay social context, manifestations of amok behavior in any form become increasingly less likely.

Suggestions for Further Investigation

Some of the limitations of this investigation were mentioned in chapter one. Certainly more comprehensive data on both the past and present occurrence of amok would be useful in assessing the validity of many of the conclusions arrived at in this study. If such data exist for the past, which seems rather doubtful, the Dutch and British colonial archives or the records of the Dutch and English East Indian companies seem the likely sources. Police, court, and hospital records especially should be carefully scrutinized.

With regard to data from the present, recent reports of amok manifestations have come from areas least penetrated by modernizing forces, Irian Jaya, and Sarawak, Papua New Guinea. Hill reports on twenty-four cases termed amok that occurred in Sarawak during the years 1954 to 1968.[1] In every case psychopathology was diagnosed, the pathology often severe in nature. Burton-Bradley's account of seven cases of amok in Papua New Guinea and what is now Irian Jaya over an eight-year period during the late 1950s and early 1960s finds no evidence of overt schizophrenia or any other type of mental disorder among the amok-runners.[2] Some of the cases reported by Hill would seem not to represent full-scale amok episodes and suggest that in this locale amok may have become a general term applied to practically any case where violent homicidal behavior is present. The occasional uses of the term in the Malaysian press during 1983-84 carried the same more generalized meaning.

The cases described by Burton-Bradley are intriguing, and it is to be hoped that records of such episodes will be kept in the coming years in Papua New Guinea and Irian Jaya as well as other areas where amok-like behavior occurs. Such records maintained over time could provide trend data useful for assessing the accuracy of the argument developed in this study regarding the demise of solitary amok in Malaysia and Indonesia. And finally, of course, if new data surfaced indicating more than scattered manifestations of both types of the amok syndrome in modern or relatively modern Malay communities then the validity of the argument certainly would be called into question.

A particularly interesting possibility for further analysis appears to lie in conducting an historical analysis of the Filipino practice of juramentado. Was the influence of Islam as central as has been suggested by Ewing and others? If so, how might we account for the contrast in this respect between the Philippines and Malaysia-Indonesia? Was juramentado or equivalent behavior sometimes employed in instances where religious motivation had little or no bearing? Has there been a resurgence of juramentado or modern variants of the pattern during the Muslim unrest pervading the southern Philippines in recent years? There also exists some evidence, largely impressionistic, that amok manifestations much like those described for Malaysia and Indonesia have been relatively common historically in the Philippines. This possibility should be further explored. The potential appears substantial for interesting and useful comparative analyses of the amok pattern across the Filipino and Malaysia-Indonesia contexts.

Finally, the historiographic approach employed in this study has proved useful in arriving at a broadened understanding of the course of amok behavior over time. This methodology will certainly prove valuable in further analyses of social phenomena and could perhaps help us to understand present-day forms of mental disorder and aberrant behavior.

Chapter 1

1. See Ralph D. Linton, <u>Culture and Mental Disorders</u> (Springfield, Ill.: Charles C. Thomas, 1956); Jane M. Murphy and Alexander H. Leighton, eds., <u>Approaches to Cross-Cultural Psychiatry</u> (Ithaca, N.Y.: Cornell Press, 1965); Marvin K. Opler, <u>Culture and Social Psychiatry</u> (New York: Atherton Press, 1967); and Stanley C. Plog and Robert B. Edgerton, eds., <u>Changing Perspectives in Mental Illness</u> (New York: Holt, Rinehart and Winston, 1969).

2. Tsung-yi Lin, "Historical Survey of Psychiatric Epidemiology in Asia," <u>Mental Hygiene</u> 47: 351-59; E. C. Wittkower, "Cultural Psychiatric Research in Asia," in <u>Mental Health Research in Asia and the Pacific</u>, eds. William Caudill and Tsung-yi Lin (Honolulu: East-West Center Press, 1969), pp. 433-47.

3. State of Perak, <u>The Perak Government Gazette</u> 4 (March 13, 1891): 131-33.

4. Howard D. Fabing, "On Going Berserk: A Neuro-chemical Inquiry," <u>Scientific Monthly</u> 83 (November 1956): 232-37.

5. Henri C. Barkley, <u>Between the Danube and the Black Sea or Five Years in Bulgaria</u> (London: John Murray, 1876), p. 313; Henry Ling Roth, <u>The Natives of Sarawak and British North Borneo</u> (London: Trustlove & Hanson, 1896). Cited by Beverly Hill, "An Investigation into Running Amok in Sarawak, Malaysia" (B.A. Thesis, Brunel College, University of London, 1970), p. 37; Clark Wissler, "Societies and Ceremonial Associations in the Oyala Division of the Teton-Hakotu," <u>Anthropological Papers of the American Museum of Natural History</u> vol. 11, part 1 (1912). Cited by Hill, "An Investigation into Running Amok in Sarawak, Malaysia," p. 37; Ruth Benedict, <u>Patterns of Culture</u> (Boston: Houghton Mifflin, 1934), p. 291; Octave J. A. Collet, <u>Terres et Peuples de</u>

Sumatra (Amsterdam: Elsevier, 1925), p. 562; Paul Radin, Indians of South America (Garden City, N.Y.: Doubleday, 1946), pp. 68-72; I. H. Coriat, "Psychoneuroses among Primitive Tribes," Journal of Abnormal and Social Psychology 10 (1915): 201. Cited by B. G. Burton-Bradley, "The Amok Syndrome in Papua and New Guinea," Medical Journal of Australia 17 (February 1968): 252.

6. B. G. Burton-Bradley, "The Amok Syndrome," pp. 252-56.

7. J. C. Zaguirre, "Amuck," Journal of the Philippine Federation of Private Medical Practitioners 6 (1957): 1138-49.

8. Philip L. Newman, "'Wild Man' Behavior in a New Guinea Highlands Community," American Anthropologist 66 (February 1964): 1-19. Cited by Burton-Bradley, "The Amok Syndrome," p. 253; Marie Reay "Mushrooms and Collective Hysteria," Australian Territories 5 (January 1965): 18-28. Cited by Burton-Bradley, "The Amok Syndrome," p. 253; L. L. Langness, "Hysterical Psychosis in the New Guinea Highlands: a Bena Bena Example?" Psychiatry 28 (1965): 258-77.

9. See Ari Kiev, "Transcultural Psychiatry Research: Problems and Perspectives," in Changing Perspectives in Mental Illness, eds. Plog and Edgerton, pp. 106-27; Opler, Culture and Social Psychiatry, pp. 114-37; and Pow Meng Yap, "The Culture-bound Reactive Syndromes," in Caudill and Lin, eds., Mental Health Research, pp. 33-53.

10. Both Alfred G. Smith, personal communication; and Kiev, "Transcultural Psychiatry," p. 124, suggest the utility of this approach.

11. An unpublished 356-item bibliography on amok, latah, and koro compiled by Alfred G. Smith proved to be an invaluable aid in the initial search for materials relevant to this investigation. Alfred G. Smith, "Bibliography of Koro, Amok, and Latah," 1957. (Mimeographed.)

Chapter 2

1. Henry Yule and A. C. Burnell, Hobson-Jobson, new ed., William Crooke ed. (London: John Murray, 1903), pp. 18-23. The etymological treatment of "a muck" in Yule and Burnell's fascinating volume provides a rich source of

information and is relied on heavily in this chapter.

2. Yule and Burnell, Hobson-Jobson, p. 19.

3. See G. W. J. Drewes, "New Light on the Coming of Islam to Indonesia?" Bijdragen tot de Taal-, Land- en Volkenkunde 124 (1968): 433-59.

4. Yule and Burnell, Hobson-Jobson, pp. 18-23.

5. Yule and Burnell, Hobson-Jobson, p. 20.

6. William Logan, Malabar (1887; reprint ed., Madras: Government Press, 1951) 1: 138.

7. Suttee involves obligatory self-sacrifice by the widow or widows of a deceased male and is normally accomplished by the widow casting herself into the funeral pyre of her husband. Suttee was a common practice in British India and occasioned substantial efforts by the British to eliminate its occurrence. Griffiths notes that economic bases existed for the practice in that relatives of the deceased and his widow(s) stood to gain economically if the wife or wives were not alive to stand in the way of distributing the man's land and resources. Thus, instances were apparently common where the widow, rather than jumping into the pyre, was pushed. Percival Griffiths, The British Impact on India (London: McDonald, 1952), pp. 216-25.

8. M. Caesar Frederike in Purchas, his Pilgrimes (1625-26) ed. S. Purchas, 2: 1708. Cited by Yule and Burnell, Hobson-Jobson, p. 20.

9. "Letter of F. Sassetti to Francesco I, Grand Duke of Tuscany," in Storia dei Viaggiatori Italiani nelle Indie Orientali, ed. Angelo de Gubernatis (Livorno: 1865), p. 154. Cited by Yule and Burnell, Hobson-Jobson, pp. 20-21.

10. Diogo de Couto, Decadas da Asia (1602; reprint ed., Lisbon: 1778), Decada IV, chap. 3, p. 1. Cited by Yule and Burnell, Hobson-Jobson, p. 21.

11. Diogo de Couto, Decadas da Asia (1614; reprint ed., Lisbon: 1778), Decada VI, chap. 8, p. 8. Cited by Yule and Burnell, Hobson-Jobson, p. 21.

12. The Travels of Pietro Della Valle in India (1650-1653; reprint ed. London: Hakluyt Society, 1892), 2: 380-81. Cited by Yule and Burnell, Hobson-Jobson, p. 21.

13. John Nieuhoff, "Mr. John Nieuhoff's Remarkable Voyages and Travels into Brazil, and the Best Parts of the East-Indies," in A Collection of

Voyages and Travels, ed. John Churchill (London: 1704), 2: 274.

14. Philip Baldaeus, "A True and Exact Description of the Most Celebrated East-India Coast of Malabar and Coromandel, and of the Island of Ceylon, with All the Adjacent Countries," in *A Collection of Voyages and Travels*, ed. Churchill, (London: 1704), 3: 644.

15. Nieuhoff, "Mr. John Nieuhoff's Remarkable Voyages," pp. 272-74.

16. Norman Chevers, *A Manual of Medical Jurisprudence for India* (Calcutta: Thacker, Spink, 1870), pp. 781-98.

17. Philip Baldaeus, "A True and Exact Description," p. 644.

18. Tome Pires, *Suma Oriental*, trans. Armando Cortesao (London: Hakluyt Society, 1944). Cited by John Bastin and Robin Winks, eds., *Malaysia: Selected Historical Readings* (Kuala Lumpur: Oxford University Press, 1966), p. 35.

19. Lady Sophia Raffles, *Memoir of the Life and Public Service of Sir Thomas Stamford Raffles* (London: James Duncan, 1835), p. 36.

20. Raffles, *Memoir*, p. 39.

21. B. Schrieke, *Indonesian Sociological Studies* (The Hague: W. van Hoeve, 1956), p. 132.

22. *Dagh-Register gehouden int Casteel Batavia 1624-1629* ('s-Gravenhage: Martinus Nijhoff, 1896), p. 67. Cited by Schrieke, *Indonesian Sociological Studies*, p. 132.

23. Cited by Schrieke, *Indonesian Sociological Studies*, p. 68.

24. J. K. J. de Jonge, ed., *De Opkomst van het Nederlandsch Gezag in Oost-Indie: Verzameling van Onuitgegevan Stukken uit het Oud-Koloniaal Archief* (Amsterdam: Frederick Muller and The Hague: Martinus Nijhoff, 1862-1909), 7: 299-302; *Dagh-Register* (1680), p. 324. Cited by Schrieke, *Indonesian Sociological Studies*, p. 133.

25. de Jonge, *Opkomst*, 8: 198-205. Cited by Schrieke, *Indonesian Sociological Studies*, p. 133.

26. Thomas Stamford Raffles, *The History of Java* (1817; reprint ed., Kuala Lumpur: Oxford University Press, 1965) 1: 298. In a footnote to this passage, Raffles adds: "It is on these occasions that the parties frequently increase their desperation by the use of opium."

27. Raffles, *History*, pp. 200-201.

28. John Crawfurd, History of the Indian Archipelago (1820; reprint ed., London: Frank Cass, 1967), 1: 67.
29. J. M. Gullick, Indigenous Political Systems of Western Malaya (London: Athlone Press, 1958), pp. 120-21.
30. Gullick, Indigenous Political Systems, p. 120.
31. Gullick, Indigenous Political Systems, p. 121.
32. Raffles, History, 1: 296-97.
33. Raffles, History, p. 259.
34. Raffles, History, p. 264. Elsewhere (p. 297), Raffles provides the following pertinent translations:

    "The brave man who has been successful in war obtains his heart's desire. The brave man who dies in war is received into heaven and cherished by the Widadaris.

    "If a man is cowardly in war and dies, the keepers of hell seize upon him in a rage:

    "Should he not die, he is reprobated and despised by all good men, even to his face."

35. Alfred Russel Wallace, The Malay Archipelago (New York: Harper and Brothers, 1869), p. 184.
36. David J. Galloway, "On Amok," in Transactions of the Fifth Biennial Congress Held at Singapore, 1923, Far Eastern Association of Tropical Medicine (London: John Bale, Sons & Danielson, 1924), p. 162.

Chapter 3

1. Hakluyt Society, "The Travels of Nicolo Conti in the East in the Early Part of the Fifteenth Century," India in the Fifteenth Century (London: Hakluyt Society, 1857), p. 16.
2. Hakluyt Society, "A Description of the Coasts of East Africa and Malabar in the Beginning of the 16th Century," Barbosa (London: Hakluyt Society, 1866), p. 194.
3. Hakluyt Society, The Voyage of Sir Henry Middleton to the Moluccas 1604-1606 (London: Hakluyt Society, 1943), p. 171.
4. Walter Schulzen, Ost-Indische Reise-Beschreibung, German edition (Amsterdam: 1676), pp. 19-20, 227. The German translation of the Dutch original rendered Wouter Schouten

as Walter Schulzen. Cited in Yule and
Burnell, <u>Hobson-Jobson</u>, p. 21.

5. KA 1883, OB 1720, Second Malacca Register,
    Missive from Governor van Suchtelen of Malacca
    to Batavia, 23 October 1720, folio 6.
6. Johan Splinter Stavorinus, <u>Voyages to the East
    Indies</u> (1798; reprint ed., London: Dawsons of
    Pall Mall, 1969) 1: 291.
7. Stavorinus, <u>Voyages</u>, pp. 291-92.
8. KA 3387, OB 1778, Perak Resident Jan Hensel to
    Malacca, 17 May 1777.
9. Perak manuscript Maxwell 24, Royal Asiatic
    Society. No further information available.
10. William Marsden, <u>The History of Sumatra</u>
    (London: 1811, 3d ed.; reprint ed., Kuala
    Lumpur: Oxford University Press, 1966), pp.
    278-9.
11. Crawfurd, <u>History</u>, 1: 67.
12. Crawfurd, <u>History</u>, 1: 69.
13. C. B. Buckley, <u>An Anecdotal History of Old
    Times in Singapore 1819-1867</u> (1902; reprint
    ed.; Kuala Lumpur: University of Malaya Press,
    1965), pp. 97-100.
14. J. R. Logan, "Malay Amoks and Piracies," in
    <u>Journal of the Indian Archipelago</u> 3 (July
    1849): 460.
15. Reprinted in Logan, "Malay Amoks," pp. 461-3.
16. W. Gilmore Ellis, "The Amok of the Malays,"
    <u>Journal of Mental Science</u> 39 (July 1893):
    331-2.
17. Sir Frank A. Swettenham, <u>The Real Malay</u>
    (London: John Lane, The Bodley Head, 1900),
    pp. 247-9.
18. Ellis, "The Amok of the Malays," pp. 322-4.
19. Sir Hugh Clifford, <u>Malayan Monochromes</u> (New
    York: E. P. Dutton, 1913), pp. 298-302.
20. John D. Gimlette, "Notes on a Case of Amok,"
    <u>Journal of Tropical Medicine</u> 4 (June 15,
    1901): 195-6, 199.
21. William Marsden, <u>A Dictionary of the Malayan
    Language</u> (London: Cox and Baylis, 1812),
    p. 16.
22. Sir Hugh Clifford and Sir Frank Swettenham,
    <u>A Dictionary of the Malay Language</u> (Taiping,
    Perak: Government Printing Office, 1894)
    p. 47. The remainder of the entry is
    instructive:

    . . . <u>Amok</u>! <u>Amok</u>! . . . Attack!
    Attack! The war cry of the Malays.
    <u>Maka kita sekelian brani marilah kita</u>

150

amok Laksamana dengan kris pandak, We
are all brave men: come, let us attack
the Laksamana with our short daggers.
Meng-amok, To attack, etc. He
Laksamana ingat-ingat karana orang
iang meng-amok itu ter-lalu banyak,
Be on thy guard, O Laksamana, for
they who are engaged in furious
conflict are very numerous. Maka ia
pun ber-tempik tiga kali berturut-
turut serta meng-amok dan menikam dan
meng-rat dengan ka-dua blah tangan,
Then he shouted three successive
times, and forthwith engaged in
furious conflict, stabbing and
slashing with both hands. Maka ia pun
meng-amok di-dalam kapal itu tiga hari
tiga malam ber-telun segala tempik
iang brani dan rioh gegak gempita ter-
lalu athamat di-dalam kapal itu tiada
sangka bunyi lagi siang dan malam
hengga sampei tiga hari tiga malam ia
meng-amok itu, He fought furiously in
that ship for three days and three
nights, shouting all manner of brave
war cries, and creating a loud and
appalling noise, which was very awe-
inspiring within the ship and which
cannot be imagined. This he did
during three days and nights, by night
and day continuing his furious
onslaught. Maka di-dalam tengah
gempar itu kadengar-an khabar-nya ka-
pada Raja Pikas Tuan Petri Ganda Eran
tunang-nya sudah mati maka ia hendak
meng-amok. In the middle of the
disturbance Raja Pikas heard that his
fiancee, the Princess Ganda Iran, was
dead, and he was about to run amok.
Maka peluru itu pun tampil-lah meng-
amok ka-pada prahu-nya iang kurang
satu s'ratus itu, The Bullets began to
rain upon his ships, which were one
hundred save one in number. Ter-lalu
kras amok Raja Petukal itu, Raja
Petukal's charge was a very violent
one. Peng-amok, One who runs amok, a
member of an attacking party, one who
engages in furious conflict. . . .

151

Chapter 4

1. John Bastin and Robin Winks, eds., Malaysia: Selected Historical Readings (Kuala Lumpur: Oxford University Press, 1966), p. 94, summarize the period of Buginese ascendancy in the Peninsula. Also see: J. Kennedy, A History of Malaya, A.D. 1400-1959 (London: Macmillan, 1962), pp. 52-66; Francis J. Moorehead, A History of Malaya (Kuala Lumpur: Longmans of Malaya, 1963), 2: 99-105; and Sir Richard Winstedt, A History of Malaya, rev. and enl. ed. (Singapore: 1962), pp. 144-48.
2. T. Oxley, "Malay Amoks," Journal of the Indian Archipelago 3 (August 1849): 533.
3. Ellis, "The Amok of the Malays," p. 326.
4. See Song Ong Siang, One Hundred Years' History of the Chinese in Malaya (1922; reprint ed., Singapore: University of Malaya Press, 1967), p. 265; David J. Galloway, "On Amok," p. 163; and "Discussion" (following paper on amok and latah), Transactions of the Fifth Biennial Congress held at Singapore, 1923, Far Eastern Association of Tropical Medicine (London: John Bale, Sons & Danielson, 1924), p. 161.
5. This appears to support the idea that amok was an infrequent event. If it had been a frequent occurrence, such behavior would have led to predictions of amok; yet there is no evidence of such a prediction ever being made correctly.
6. Logan, "Malay Amoks," pp. 463-64.
7. Sir Hugh Clifford, The Further Side of Silence (New York: Doubleday, Page, 1922), pp. 320-21. Clifford continues with an example from his experience.

> In the year 1888 I spent two nights awake by the side of Raja Haji Hamid, who was on the verge of such a nervous outbreak; and it was only by bringing to bear every atom of moral influence as I had over him, that I was able to restrain him from running amok in the streets of Pekan, the capital of Pahang, because his father had died a natural death on the other side of the peninsula, and because the then Sultan of Selangor had behaved with characteristic parsimony in the matter of his funeral. He had no quarrel with

the people of Pahang, but his liver
was sick, and the weariness of life
which this condition of mind
engendered impelled him to kill all
and sundry, until he himself should,
in his turn, be killed.

8. Ellis, "The Amok of the Malays," p. 336.
9. William Fletcher, "Latah and Amok," in The
    British Encyclopedia of Medical Practice, ed.
    Sir Humphrey Rolleston (London: Butterworth
    and Co., 1938), p. 649; Ellis, "The Amok of
    the Malays" and "Some Remarks on Asylum
    Practice in Singapore," Journal of Tropical
    Medicine 4 (December 1901): 413; and Oxley,
    "Malay Amoks," p. 532.
10. Ellis, "Some Remarks on Asylum Practice in
    Singapore"; and Tassilo Adam, "Amok and Mata
    Gelap--Other Malay Diseases," Knickerbocker
    Weekly 8 (April 1946): 20.
11. Ellis, "The Amok of the Malays," p. 335.
12. Oxley, "Malay Amoks," p. 532.
13. In this regard, it is interesting to note
    that those Malay Muslims in the southern
    Philippines who committed juramentado with its
    multiple homicidal aggressive acts of unparal-
    leled fury and frenzy, did discriminate in
    their choice of victims to a certain extent.
    Their acts were aimed only at non-Muslims in
    this highly institutionalized, ritualistic and
    ultimately suicidal effort which was thought
    to assure passage to a nirvanic afterlife.
    J. Franklin Ewing, "Juramentado: Institu-
    tionalized Suicide Among the Moros of the
    Philippines," Anthropological Quarterly 28
    (October 1955): 148-55.
14. Agnes Newton Keith, Land Below the Wind
    (Boston: Little, Brown, 1944), pp. 139-57.
    Keith relates in detail the 1935 amok of a
    Malay, Abanawas, in British North Borneo. The
    probably semi-fictional episode she describes
    bears most of the characteristics of a classic
    case of amok except that Abanawas selects the
    rifle as his sole weapon and ensconces himself
    in a guard tower where, before succumbing to a
    fusillade of bullets, he fires at will at
    members of the Semporna populace. This
    removal of the self from the immediate
    physical proximity of his victims or potential
    victims is not at all characteristic of the
    Malay amok-runner. This case, probably

emanating at least in part from the imagination of a talented Western author, is the only one reviewed in this investigation where the amok-runner makes use of firearms.

15. Ellis, "The Amok of the Malays," p. 326.
16. The same phenomenon appears to have occurred among those engaging in _juramentado_ in the Southern Philippines. With the presence of gun-runners and the American military near the beginning of the twentieth century, these individuals probably had ready access to firearms. Yet there is no indication of any use being made of such weaponry in _juramentado_ attacks.
17. Clifford, _The Further Side of Silence_, p. 320.
18. Sir Frank A. Swettenham, _British Malaya_ (London: 1907; new ed., London: 1948), p. 135. Cited by Gullick, _Indigenous Political Systems_, p. 123.
19. T. J. Newbold, _British Settlements in the Straits of Malacca_ (London: John Murray, 1839), 2: 185.
20. Logan, "Malay Amoks and Piracies," p. 464. Logan suggests that "a state of society which requires every individual to be ready at any time to use his _kris_ is quite inconsistent with a horror of shedding blood."
21. Galloway, "On Amok," p. 168.
22. Raffles, _History_, 1: 352. Oxley, "Malay Amoks," p. 532, echoes the comments of Raffles:

> What has so often been written of their revengeful spirit is much exaggerated; polite in the extreme according to their own ideas, they never indulge in abuse one towards the other, the only reply to any deviation from this rule is the Kriss, for which they will watch their opportunity and most certainly not afford their adversary any advantage if is in their power to deprive him of. This is their code of honour, and being fully aware of it amongst themselves, provocation is seldom given, and satisfaction as seldom required.

23. Gullick, _Indigenous Political Systems_, p. 122.
24. Gullick, _Indigenous Political Systems_, pp. 122-23.

25. Gullick, Indigenous Political Systems, p. 123.
26. See G. C. Woolley, "The Malay Keris, Its Origin and Development," Journal Malayan Branch Royal Asiatic Society 20, pt. 2 (1947): 60-104; A. E. Coope, "The Floating Cannon of Butterworth," Journal Malayan Branch Asiatic Society 20, pt. 1 (1947): 18-33; and W. H. Rassers, "On the Javanese Kris," Bijdragen tot de Taal-, Land- en Volkenkunde van Nederlandsch-Indie 99 (1940): 501-83.
27. Gullick, Indigenous Political Systems, p. 123.
28. F. M. Schnitger, Forgotten Kingdoms in Sumatra (London: E. J. Brill, 1964), pp. 29-30, provides an interesting example from Sumatra.
29. Gimlette, "Notes on a Case of Amok," p. 198.
30. Swettenham, The Real Malay, pp. 246-47.
31. Raffles, History, 2, app. C: xlvii.
32. Newbold, British Settlements, 2: 237.
33. Isabella L. Bird, The Golden Chersonese (1883; reprint ed., Kuala Lumpur: Oxford University Press, 1967), pp. 356-57.
34. John Frederick A. McNair, Perak and the Malays, reprint ed., Kuala Lumpur: Oxford University Press, 1972, pp. 213-16.
35. Sir Richard Winstedt, The Malays: A Cultural History, 6th ed. (London: Routledge & Kegan Paul, 1961), pp. 91-2.
36. Winstedt, The Malays, pp. 80-81.
37. R. J. Wilkinson, "Malay Law," in Papers on Malay Subjects, ed. R. J. Wilkinson (Kuala Lumpur: F.M.S. Government Printer, 1908), p. 3.
38. A copy of adat law as applicable in one area of Sumatra in 1807 is quoted by Marsden, with the section on murder, wounding, and assault illustrative of the institution of bangun. Marsden, History, p. 234.
39. Winstedt, The Malays, p. 78.
40. In Marsden's compilation of Sumatran adat law cited above (note 38) is found a section on outlawry followed by Marsden's own comments. Marsden, History, pp. 220-21, 237, 246.
41. Marsden, History, pp. 247-48.
42. Newbold, British Settlements, 2: 237-38.
43. Newbold, British Settlements, p. 237.
44. Winstedt, The Malays, pp. 70, 109.
45. Ellis, "The Amok of the Malays," p. 326.
46. Raffles, History, 1: 250, 287-89; Stavorinus, Voyages, 1: 288; and Donald Maclaine Campbell, Java: Past and Present (London: William Heinemann, 1915), 2: 1073-78. In Dagh-

Register gehouden int Casteel Batavia, can be found running accounts of cases disposed of before the Court of Justice of Batavia and the severe punishments inflicted in individual cases.

47. Stavorinus, *Voyages*, 1: 292.
48. Stavorinus, *Voyages*, p. 294.
49. Stavorinus, *Voyages*, p. 292.
50. Stavorinus, *Voyages*, pp. 288-89.
51. Stavorinus, *Voyages*, p. 292.
52. Clive Day, *The Dutch in Java* (1904; reprint ed., Kuala Lumpur: Oxford University Press, 1966), pp. 153-54. Day summarizes well the shortcomings of Dutch judicial organization under the Dutch East India Company.
53. Stavorinus, *Voyages*, 1: 294.
54. Day, *The Dutch in Java*, p. 154, notes that during the 1799-1911 period between the fall of the Company and the assumption of rule by the British,

> Daendels took the only step adapted to remedy this state of affairs, by increasing the number of courts, making each prefect the president of a native tribunal, in which all civil and criminal cases, unless they were of unusual moment, were tried. . . . Daendels also increased the number of high courts and ordered that native courts should meet twice a week in each regency.

As for the impact of Raffles and the British, Day (p. 195) notes as follows:

> The judicial reorganization by Raffles is . . . one of the best and most permanent results of the period of British rule. Raffles made a clean sweep of the previous arrangements for the administration of justice and reestablished them with an eye both to the general principles underlying judicial efficiency, and to the local needs of Europeans and natives in various districts. He found that no distinction was made in the exercise of police and properly judicial functions, that abuses which he termed scandalous still existed in the

conduct of justice, and that the
system of courts was badly arranged.
The measures which he took were far
from remedying all evils, and he made
some serious blunders, as in the
attempt to introduce the British jury
system into native Java. There seems
no question, however, that he rendered
the administration of justice for
Europeans more efficient, and that he
established the principles on which
the judicial relations with the
natives were afterward developed.

55. Raffles, History, 1: 287-90.
56. Raffles, History, p. 250.
57. See B. ter Haar, "Western Influence on the Law
for the Native Population," in The Effect of
Western Influence on Native Civilizations in
the Malay Archipelago, ed. B. Schrieke
(Batavia: G. Kolff, 1929), pp. 158-70. Ter
Haar notes (p. 161):

If . . . we . . . review the penal
law, it appears that the Western law
occupies first place in regard to the
native population as well as the
Europeans. The penal code . . . is
almost an exact copy of the Dutch
penal code. . . . If we enquire as to
the specifically Western characteristics of this penal code, it is found
primarily in the penalties. . . . The
majority of offenses are also recognized by the adat law as such but the
punishment by imprisonment is seldom
or never used as a corrective. As
such, it is therefore an important
Western element introduced in the law
for the native population.

58. See Dirk Schoute, Occidental Therapeutics in
the Netherlands East Indies During Three
Centuries of Netherlands Settlement (1600-
1900) (Batavia: Netherlands Indian Public
Health Service, 1937), pp. 164-67. Schoute
reports that at least through the first half
of the nineteenth century the Chinese hospital
of Batavia represented the primary and almost
sole institutional provision for the mentally
ill from both inside and outside Java. Small

departments for handling the insane, primarily soldiers, were added to the military hospitals in Batavia (1832-1836) and Semarang (1849). In 1875 a decree was issued authorizing the erection of a central asylum at Buitenzorg, and of two auxiliary hospitals at Semarang and at Surabaya. Later on, the two auxiliary hospitals were replaced by one central institution near Malang. At the time Schoute writes, the institutions at Buitenzorg and near Malang continued to be among the most important asylums in Netherlands India.

59. F. H. van Loon, "Acute Confusional Insanity in the Dutch East Indies, Mededeelingen van den Burgerlijken Geneeskundigenn Dienst in Nederlandsch-Indie pt. 4 (1922): 202.
60. Schoute, Occidental Therapeutics, p. 165.
61. F. H. van Loon, "Acute Confusional Insanity in the Dutch East Indies," p. 202.
62. Linton, Culture and Mental Disorders, p. 116.
63. Carl A. Bock, The Head-Hunters of Borneo, 2d ed. (London: Sampson, Low, Marston, Searle & Rivington, 1882), p. 257.
64. Buckley, Anecdotal History, p. 103.
65. Buckley, Anecdotal History, p. 115.
66. Buckley, Anecdotal History, pp. 97-100.
67. George Windson Earl, The Eastern Seas or Voyages and Adventures in the Indian Archipelago in 1932-33-34 (London: William H. Allen, 1837), pp. 377-78.
68. Journal of the Eastern Archipelago 3 (July 1849): 460-63.
69. Ellis, "The Amok of the Malays," p. 329; and Gimlette, "Notes on a Case of Amok," p. 197.
70. John Cameron, Our Tropical Possessions in Malayan India (London: 1865; reprint ed., Kuala Lumpur: Oxford University Press, 1965), pp. 261-62. During the 1850s in southern India the British administration also found it necessary to respond to amok-running or what might be more properly termed multiple homicide. Combing court reports for this period, Chevers relates twelve cases identified as amok where the perpetrator is captured and adjudicated in British courts. A death sentence is imposed in five cases, transportation for life in four cases, no final disposition is reported in two cases, and in the final case the perpetrator dies of opium poisoning before the case can be tried.

Chevers, A Manual of Medical Jurisprudence for India, pp. 781-93.

71. Buckley, Anecdotal History, p. 703.

72. Charles G. Garrard, comp., The Acts and Ordinances of the Legislative Council of the Straits Settlements: From the 1st April 1967 to the 7th March 1898 (London: Eyre and Spottiswoode, 1898), especially Ordinance No. IV of 1871, "The Penal Code," 1: 86-87, 140-45; and A. B. Voules, comp., The Laws of the Federated Malay States: 1877-1920 (London: Hazell, Watson & Viney, 1921), especially "Criminal Procedure Code," 1: 292-93, 352-53.

73. Garrard, The Acts and Ordinances of the Legislative Council of the Straits Settlements, 1: 141. This statement is followed by these provisions:

> First--That the provocation is not sought or voluntarily provoked by the offender as an excuse for killing or doing harm to any person.
>
> Secondly--That the provocation is not given by anything done in obedience to the law, or by a public servant in the lawful exercise of the powers of such public servant.
>
> Thirdly--That the provocation is not given by anything done in the lawful exercise of the right of private defence.

74. Voules, Laws, 1: 352.

75. Garrard, Acts and Ordinances, 1: 142-43. The complete sections read:

> Culpable homicide is not murder if the offender, in the exercise in good faith of the right of private defence of person or property, exceeds the power given to him by law, and causes the death of the person against whom he is exercising such right of defence, without premeditation and without any intention of doing more harm than is necessary for the purpose of such defence. . . .

Culpable homicide is not murder if the offender, being a public servant, or aiding a public servant acting for the advancement of the public justice, exceeds the powers given to him by law, and causes death by doing an act which he, in good faith, believes to be lawful and necessary for the due discharge of his duty as such public servant, and without ill-will towards the person whose death is caused.

76. Voules, <u>Laws</u>, p. 292.
77. Voules, <u>Laws</u>, p. 292.
78. Voules, <u>Laws</u>, p. 292.
79. Voules, <u>Laws</u>, p. 293.
80. Voules, <u>Laws</u>, p. 293.
81. William G. Maxwell, comp., <u>The Laws of Perak, from the 11th September, 1877 to the 31st December 1903</u> (Kuala Lumpur: 1907).
82. Gimlette, "Notes on a Case of Amok," p. 196.
83. Gimlette, "Notes on a Case of Amok," p. 196.
84. McNair, <u>Perak and the Malays: Sarong and Kris</u>, p. 214.
85. Ellis, "The Amok of the Malays," p. 326.
86. Ellis, Medical Superintendent at the Government Asylum in Singapore, provides an interesting commentary on conditions in the asylum upon his arrival in 1888. Ellis, "Some Remarks on Asylum Practice in Singapore," pp. 411-12.

On arriving here . . . to take up my post . . . it seemed to me that I had gone back a hundred years at least. No casebooks; no medical journals; no <u>post-mortem</u> records. A register did exist, but the names of patients were unknown; the register and the numbers of the patients agreed, but that was all. There was a palatial [sic] asylum, badly drained and worse ventilated, mostly built in blocks of ten single rooms. . . . Fixed bedsteads were placed throughout immediately below barred windows; proper supervision was difficult. . . . Strait-jackets were in evidence, and all criminal lunatics and lunatic criminals were in leg irons. Added to the above,

one had to contend with quite a
babel of tongues, for four dialects
of Chinese, Malay, Tamil,
Hindustani, and Javanese were
commonly spoken; and Burmese,
Japanese, Siamese, Annamite, and
several different Eastern Archipelago islanders, speaking but their
own language, were all represented
in the 200 odd patients I found
awaiting me.

Descriptive rolls sent by the
police with new patients are in many
instances wrongly filled up, the
answers in no way applying to the
questions. The majority of the cases
are wandering lunatics in, as is to be
expected, the poorest of physical
condition, and about whom no history
can be gleaned.

87. Gimlette, "Notes on a Case of Amok," p. 197.
88. Gimlette, "Notes on a Case of Amok," p. 197.
89. R. Desmond Fitzgerald, "A Thesis on Two
Tropical Neuroses (Amok and Latah) Peculiar to
Malaya," in Transactions of the Fifth Biennial
Congress held at Singapore, 1923, Far Eastern
Association of Tropical Medicine (London: John
Bale, Sons & Danielson, 1924), p. 161.
90. Annual Departmental Reports of the Straits
Settlements (Singapore: Government Printing
Office).

1899, pp. 419, 421.   1909, p. 36.
1900, p. 161.   1912, p. 347.
1908, p. 95.   1918, p. 77.

Federated Malay States. Reports 1900.
(London: Darling & Son) report for Pahang,
p. 87.

Protected Malay States. Reports 1890.
(London: Eyre and Spottiswoode), p. 51.

91. Marsden, History, p. 279.
92. Marsden, History, p. 280.
93. Crawfurd, History, 1: 66.
94. Buckley, Anecdotal History, p. 112.
95. Journal of the Indian Archipelago 3 (July
1849): 461.

96. Oxley, "Malay Amoks," p. 532. Oxley's statement is not clear and might be interpreted differently than it is here. The relevant passage reads:

> For instance a man sitting quietly amongst his friends and relatives will, without provocation, suddenly start up weapon in hand and slay all within his reach. I have known so many as 8 killed and wounded by a very feeble individual in this manner. Next day when interrogated whether he was not sorry for the act he had committed, no one could be more contrite; when asked why then did you do it, the answer has invariably been "the Devil entered into me, my eyes were darkened, I did not know what I was about." I have received this reply on at least twenty different occasions. . . .

Rather than referring to twenty separate amok episodes, the meaning may be that a given amok-runner continued to give this response during as many as twenty questionings about a single amok episode. However, shortly after this passage, Oxley makes the previously cited statement that three-fourths of the cases of amok with which he was familiar were carried out by Buginese. One normally would not use a proportion such as three-fourths unless the numerical referent was more than a small number of cases. It is primarily on this basis that the conclusion is drawn that Oxley had substantial contact with amok and that "twenty different occasions" is probably at least roughly indicative of the number of individual cases with which he was familiar.

97. Wallace, The Malay Archipelago, p. 184.
98. Bird, The Golden Chersonese, p. 356.
99. Bird, The Golden Chersonese, p. 256.
100. Ellis, "The Amok of the Malays," p. 326.
101. Clifford and Swettenham, A Dictionary of the Malay Language, p. 48.
102. Swettenham, The Real Malay, p. 253.
103. Gimlette, Dictionary, p. 142; Gimlette, "Notes on a Case of Amok," p. 198; Buckley, Anecdotal History, pp. 100, 500; Van Loon "Acute Confusional Insanity," p. 214; Galloway, "On

Amok," p. 171; Fitzgerald, "Thesis," p. 153; Fletcher, "Latah and Amok," p. 648; and Yap, "Culture-bound."

104. Earl, The Eastern Seas or Voyages and Adventures in the Indian Archipelago in 1932-33-34, p. 377.
105. Clifford, The Further Side of Silence, p. 319.
106. Stavorinus, Voyages, 1: 292.
107. Ellis, "The Amok of the Malays," p. 326.
108. Raffles, History, 1: 355; McNair, Perak and the Malays: Sarong and Kris, pp. 214-15; Bird, The Golden Chersonese, pp. 165, 357; Crawfurd, History, 1: 67-68. One of these devices may be seen today in the Musim Negara in Kuala Lumpur.

Chapter 5

1. See Fabing, "On Going Berserk: A Neurochemical Inquiry," Scientific Monthly 83 (November 1951): 232-37; and Marie Reay, "Mushroom Madness in the New Guinea Highlands," Oceania 31 (1960): 135-39.
2. See citation from Cook's Voyages in Oxford English Dictionary (London: Oxford University Press 1933), 1: 95; W. Cool, With the Dutch in the East: An Outline of the Military Operations in Lombock, 1894 (London: Luzac and Co., 1897), p. 104; reference to the work of S. L. Leymann in Fitzgerald, "A Thesis on Two Tropical Neuroses (Amok and Latah) Peculiar to Malaya," p. 149; and the citation of Hogendorp's views in Raffles, History, pp. 103-4.
3. Cameron, Our Tropical Possessions in Malayan India, p. 261.
4. Cases of insanity were often linked to the use of opium. For a description and critical analysis showing little if any support for this view, see David J. Galloway "Opium Smoking," in Transactions of the Fifth Biennial Congress held at Singapore, 1923, Far Eastern Association of Tropical Medicine (London: John Bale, Sons & Danielson, 1924), pp. 864-85; and Ellis, "Some Remarks on Asylum Practice in Singapore," pp. 411-14.
5. Marsden, History, p. 278.
6. Chevers, Manual, pp. 781-98.
7. Chevers, Manual, pp. 789-95.

8. Cited by van Loon, "Acute Confusional Insanity in the Dutch East Indies," p. 206.

9. Jal Edulji Dhunjibhoy, "A Brief Resume of the Types of Insanity Commonly Met with in India, with a Full Description of 'Indian Hemp Insanity' Peculiar to the Country," Journal of Mental Science 76 (April 1930): 254-64.

10. Dhunjibhoy, "Resume," p. 261.

11. Marsden, History, pp. 278-79.

12. As cited in F. H. van Loon, "Amok and Lattah," Journal of Abnormal Psychology 21 (1927): 436.

13. Fitzgerald, "A Thesis on Two Tropical Neuroses (Amok and Latah) Peculiar to Malaya," p. 151.

14. Gimlette, "Notes on a Case of Amok," p. 198.

15. Van Loon, "Acute Confusional Insanity in the Dutch East Indies," p. 215.

16. Van Loon, "Amok and Lattah," p. 436.

17. Fletcher, "Latah and Amok," p. 648.

18. Fitzgerald, "A Thesis on Two Tropical Neuroses (Amok and Latah) Peculiar to Malaya," p. 152.

19. Van Loon, "Acute Confusional Insanity in the Dutch East Indies," p. 219.

20. Galloway, "On Amok," pp. 165-66.

21. Galloway, "On Amok," pp. 165-67.

22. Fletcher, "Latah and Amok," p. 648.

23. Wan A. Hamid, "Religion and Culture of the Modern Malay," in Malaysia, ed. Wang Gungwu (London: Pall Mall Press, 964), p. 183.

24. Ewing, "Juramentado: Institutionalized Suicide Among the Moros of the Philippines," p. 150.

25. Ewing, "Juramentado," p. 154.

26. Ewing, "Juramentado," p. 154.

27. Ellis, "The Amok of the Malays," pp. 329-31.

28. Cited by Swettenham, The Real Malay, p. 234.

29. Gimlette, "Notes on a Case of Amok," p. 198.

30. Van Loon, "Amok and Lattah," p. 437.

31. Van Loon, "Amok and Lattah," pp. 437-38.

32. Galloway, "On Amok," p. 168.

33. Galloway, "On Amok," p. 170.

34. Pow Meng Yap, "Mental Diseases Peculiar to Certain Cultures: A Survey of Comparative Psychiatry," Journal of Mental Science 97 (April 1951): 320.

35. Gimlette, "Notes on a Case of Amok," p. 197; Fletcher, "Latah and Amok," p. 648.

36. Fletcher, "Latah and Amok," p. 648.

37. Summarized in Fletcher, "Latah and Amok."

38. A. F. C. Wallace, "Culture Change and Mental Illness," in Changing Perspectives in Mental Illness, ed. Plog and Edgerton, p. 82.

39. Gullick, Indigenous Political Systems, p. 138.

40. Kiev, "Transcultural Psychiatry: Research Problems and Perspectives," p. 106.

Chapter 6

1. C. D. Cowan argues that the British decision to take action in Malaya was not provoked by "conditions in the peninsula, nor by any consideration of British economic interests there but by fear of foreign intervention. . . . The promotion of British economic interests in the area . . . has in fact always been secondary to the defense of India, the protection of the sea route to China, and the denial of bases along that route to potentially dangerous powers." C. D. Cowan, <u>Nineteenth-Century Malaya: The Origins of British Political Control</u>, reprinted in part in <u>Malaysia: Selected Historical Readings</u>, eds. Bastin and Winks, p. 188. The ultimate reasons for intervention in either Indonesia or Malaysia are of little consequence to the present analysis. Whatever the reasons, the impact remains.
2. Gullick, <u>Indigenous Political Systems</u>. The elaborate detail of Gullick's work has been summarized succinctly by William R. Roff, <u>The Origins of Malay Nationalism</u> (New Haven: Yale University Press 1967), pp. 1-11. The discussion which follows relies on both original and the summarization by Roff.
3. Roff, <u>Origins</u>, p. 4.
4. Roff, <u>Origins</u>, pp. 5-6.
5. Roff, <u>Origins</u>, p. 5.
6. J. M. Gullick, <u>Malaya</u> (New York: Praeger, 1963).
7. Roff, <u>Origins</u>, pp. 6-7.
8. Roff, <u>Origins</u>, p. 10.
9. Raffles, <u>History</u>, 1: 232.
10. Raffles, <u>History</u>, p. 294.
11. Abdullah bin Abdul Kadir, <u>The Story of the Voyage of Abdullah bin Abdul Kadir, Munshi</u>, trans. A. E. Coope (Singapore: 1949), reprinted in part in <u>Malaysia, Selected Historical Readings</u>, eds. Bastin and Winks, pp. 149-50 (see also pp. 142, 145).
12. Harry Miller, <u>A Short History of Malaysia</u> (New York: Praeger, 1966), pp. 95-96.
13. Miller, <u>History</u>, p. 105.
14. Winstedt, <u>The Malays</u>, pp. 120-21.

15. Miller, History, p. 131.
16. Gullick, Malaya, p. 33.
17. Especially useful sources in this area are Swettenham, British Malaya, reprinted in part in Malaysia: Selected Historical Readings, eds. Bastin and Winks; C. N. Parkinson, British Intervention in Malaya, 1867-1877 (Singapore: 1960); and Cowan, Nineteenth Century Malaya.
18. Roff, Origins, p. 18.
19. Roff, Origins, pp. 18-19.
20. Roff, Origins, p. 20.
21. Winstedt, The Malays, pp. 80-81.
22. Gullick, Malaya, p. 57.
23. Gullick, Malaya, pp. 45-46.
24. D. G. E. Hall, A History of South-East Asia, 2d ed. (London: Macmillan, 1964), pp. 532-33.
25. Gullick, Malaya, p. 49.
26. Hall, History, p. 534.
27. Gullick, Malaya, p. 58.
28. Roff, Origins, pp. 30-31.
29. The Culture System as initiated under Governor-General Johannes van den Bosch is described in Hall, History, pp. 516-19.
30. Hall, History, p. 544.
31. Bernard H. M. Vlekke, Nusantara: A History of Indonesia, rev. ed. (The Hague: W. van Hoeve, 1960), p. 315.
32. Vlekke, Nusantara, p. 328.
33. Nicholas Tarling, A Concise History of Southeast Asia (New York: Praeger, 1966), p. 169.
34. A section which follows, describing the primary features and impact of the "Ethical Policy" draws heavily on Herbert Feith, "Indonesia," in Governments and Politics of Southeast Asia, ed. George McT. Kahin, 2d ed. (Ithaca, N.Y.: Cornell University Press, 1964), pp. 191-93.
35. Hall, History, p. 706, summarizes the Dutch effort to use the village as the lever for the improvement of native welfare thusly:

> The most elaborate village administration was built up. But it was an instrument for such excessive interference from above that there was hardly any village autonomy left, and the general effect was to turn villages against Dutch rule. The Dutch method has been described by Mr.

Furnivall a "Let me help you, let me
show you how to do it, let me do it
for you."

36. John Bastin and Harry J. Benda, A History of
Modern Southeast Asia (Englewood Cliffs, N.J.:
Prentice-Hall, 1968), p. 87.
37. The failures were due in part to European
opposition to the "Ethical Policy."   Tarling,
History, p. 175.
38. David J. Steinberg, ed., In Search of
Southeast Asia (New York: Praeger, 1971),
p. 281.
39. Roff, Origins, p. 30.

Chapter 7

1. Hill, "An Investigation into Running Amok in
Sarawak, Malaysia."
2. Burton-Bradley, "The Amok Syndrome in Papua
and New Guinea."

BIBLIOGRAPHY

Abdullah bin Abdul Kadir. The Story of the Voyage of Abdullah bin Abdul Kadir, Munshi. Trans. by A. E. Coope. Singapore: 1949. Cited in Bastin and Winks, Malaysia.

Adam, Tassilo. "Amok and Mata Gelap--Other Malay Diseases," Knickerbocker Weekly 8 (April 1946): pp. 18-21.

Allen, J. de V. "Two Imperialists: A Study of Sir Frank Swettenham and Sir Hugh Clifford," Journal Malayan Branch Royal Asiatic Society 37 (1964): 41-73.

Annual Departmental Reports of the Straits Settlements. Singapore: Government Printing Office, 1899, 1900, 1908-9, 1912, 1918.

Baring-Gould, Sabine and Bampfylde, C. A. A History of Sarawak under its Two White Rajahs 1839-1908. London: Henry Sotheran & Co., 1909.

Barkley, Henri C. Between the Danube and the Black Sea or Five Years in Bulgaria. London: John Murray, 1876.

Bastin, John and Benda, Harry J. A History of Modern Southeast Asia. Englewood Cliffs, N.J.: Prentice-Hall, 1968.

Bastin, John and Winks, Robin, eds. Malaysia: Selected Historical Readings. Kuala Lumpur: Oxford University Press, 1966.

Becker, Howard S., ed. The Other Side: Perspectives on Deviance. New York: Free Press of Glencoe, 1964.

Benedict, Ruth. Patterns of Culture. Boston: Houghton Mifflin, 1934.

Bird, Isabella L. The Golden Chersonese. 1883; reprint ed., Kuala Lumpur: Oxford University Press, 1967.

Bock, Carl A. The Head-Hunters of Borneo. 2d ed. London: Sampson, Low, Marston, Searle & Rivington, 1882.

Bohannan, Paul. "Theories of Homicide and Suicide." In African Homicide and Suicide, pp. 3-29. Princeton, N.J.: Princeton University Press, 1960.

Boyle, Frederick. _Adventures Among the Dyaks of Borneo_. London: Hurst and Blackett, 1865.

Buckley, C. B. _An Anecdotal History of Old Times in Singapore 1819-1867_. 1902; reprint ed., Kuala Lumpur: University of Malaya Press, 1965.

Burton-Bradley, B. G. "The Amok Syndrome in Papua and New Guinea," _Medical Journal of Australia_, 17 February 1968: pp. 252-56.

Caesar Frederike, M. in _Purchas, his Pilgrimes (1625-26)_ ed. S. Purchas, 2: 1708. Cited by Yule and Burnell, _Hobson-Jobson_.

Cameron, John. _Our Tropical Possessions in Malayan India_. London: 1865; reprint ed., Kuala Lumpur: Oxford University Press, 1965.

Campbell, Donald Maclaine. _Java: Past and Present_. 2 vols. London: William Heinemann, 1915.

Caudill, William and Lin, Tsung-yi, eds. _Mental Health Research in Asia and the Pacific_. Honolulu: East-West Center Press, 1969.

Chevers, Norman. _A Manual of Medical Jurisprudence for India_. Calcutta: Thacker, Spink & Co., 1870.

Chijs, J. A. van der. _Nederlandsch-Indisch Plakaatboek, 1602-1811_. 16 vols. 's-Gravenhage: Martinus Nijhoff, 1890.

Clifford, Sir Hugh. _The Further Side of Silence_. New York: Doubleday, Page & Co., 1922.

_____. _Malayan Monochromes_. New York: E. P. Dutton & Co., 1913.

Clifford, Sir Hugh and Swettenham, Sir Frank A. _A Dictionary of the Malay Language_. Taiping, Perak: Government Printing Office, 1894.

Collet, Octave J. A. _Terres et Peuples de Sumatra_. Amsterdam: Elsevier, 1925.

Cool, W. _With the Dutch in the East: An Outline of the Military Operations in Lombock, 1894_. London: Luzac & Co., 1897.

Coriat, I. H. "Psychoneuroses among Primitive Tribes," _Journal of Abnormal and Social Psychology_ 10 (1915): 201. Cited by B. G. Burton-Bradley, "The Amok Syndrome in Papua and New Guinea," _Medical Journal of Australia_ 17 (February 1968): 252.

Couto, Diogo de. _Decadas da Asia_. 1602; reprint ed., Lisbon: 1778. , Decada IV, chap. 3, p. 1. Cited by Yule and Burnell, _Hobson-Jobson_.

Cowan, C. D. _Nineteenth-Century Malaya: The Origins of British Political Control_, reprinted in part in _Malaysia: Selected Historical Readings_. Edited by John Bastin and Robin Winks.

Crawfurd, John. A Descriptive Dictionary of the Indian Islands and Adjacent Countries. London: Bradbury & Evans, 1856.

_____. History of the Indian Archipelago. 3 vols. 1820; reprint ed., London: Frank Cass & Co., 1967.

Dagh-Register gehouden int Casteel Batavia. s'-Gravenhage: Martinus Nijhoff, 1896.

Day, Clive. The Dutch in Java. 1904; reprint ed., Kuala Lumpur: Oxford University Press, 1966.

De Jonge, J. K. J. (Jr.), ed. De Opkomst van het Nederlandsch Gezag in Oost-Indie: Verzameling van Onuitgegeven Stukken uit het Oud-Koloniaal Archief. 7 vols. Amsterdam: Frederick Muller and The Hague: Martinus Nijhoff, 1862-1909.

Dentan, R. K. "Semai Response to Mental Aberration," Bijdragen tot de Taal-, Land- en Volkenkunde 124 (1968): 135-58.

Dhunjibhoy, Jal Edulji. "A Brief Resumé of the Types of Insanity Commonly Met with in India, with a Full Description of 'Indian Hemp Insanity' Peculiar to the Country," Journal of Mental Science 76 (April 1930): 254-64.

Drewes, G. W. J. "New Light on the Coming of Islam to Indonesia?" Bijdragen tot de Taal-, Land- en Volkenkunde 124 (1968): 433-59.

DuBois, Cora. The People of Alor: A Socio-Psychological Study of an East Indian Island. Cambridge, Mass.: Harvard University Press, 1960.

Durkheim, Emile. Suicide: A Study in Sociology. Trans. John A. Spaulding and George Simpson. Edited with an Introduction by George Simpson. Glencoe, Ill.: The Free Press, 1951.

Earl, George Windson. The Eastern Seas or Voyages and Adventures in the Indian Archipelago in 1932-33-34. London: William H. Allen & Co., 1837.

Ellis, W. Gilmore. "The Amok of the Malays," Journal of Mental Science 39 (July 1893): 325-38.

_____. "Some Remarks on Asylum Practice in Singapore," Journal of Tropical Medicine 4 (December 1901): 413.

Endicott, Kirk Michael. An Analysis of Malay Magic. London: Oxford University Press, 1970.

Erikson, Kai T. Wayward Puritans: A Study in the Sociology of Deviance. New York: John Wiley & Sons, 1966.

Ewing, J. Franklin. "Juramentado: Institutionalized Suicide Among the Moros of the Philippines,"

Anthropological Quarterly 28 (October 1955):
148-55.
Fabing, Howard D. "On Going Berserk: A Neuro-
chemical Inquiry," Scientific Monthly 83
(November 1956): 232-37.
Fauconnier, Henri. The Soul of Malaya. Trans. Eric
Sutton. London: 1931; reprint ed., Kuala
Lumpur: Oxford University Press, 1965.
Federated Malay States: Annual Reports. London:
Darling & Son, 1900.
Feith, Herbert. "Indonesia." In Governments and
Politics of Southeast Asia, pp. 183-278.
Edited by George McT. Kahin. Ithaca, N.Y.:
Cornell University Press, 1964.
Fisher, Charles A. Southeast Asia: A Social,
Economic and Political Geography. 2d ed.
London: Methuen & Co., 1966.
Fitzgerald, R. Desmond. "A Thesis on Two Tropical
Neuroses (Amok and Latah) Peculiar to Malaya."
In Transactions of the Fifth Biennial Congress
held at Singapore, 1923. Far Eastern
Association of Tropical Medicine, pp. 148-60.
London: John Bale, Sons & Danielson, 1924.
Fletcher, William. "Latah and Amok." In British
Encyclopedia of Medical Practice, vol. 7, pp.
641-50. 9 vols. Edited by Sir Humphrey
Rolleston. London: Butterworth & Co., 1938.
Frazer, J. G. The Golden Bough: A Study in Magic
and Religion. 3d edition. London: Macmillan
& Co., 1911.
Furnivall, J. S. Colonial Policy and Practice: A
Comparative Study of Burma and Netherlands
India. Cambridge: Cambridge University Press,
1948.
Galloway, David J. "On Amok." In Transactions of
the Fifth Biennial Congress held at Singapore,
1923. Far Eastern Association of Tropical
Medicine, pp. 162-71. London: John Bale, Sons
& Danielson, 1924.
_____. "Opium Smoking." In Transactions of the
Fifth Biennial Congress held at Singapore,
1923. Far Eastern Association of Tropical
Medicine, pp. 864-85. London: John Bale, Sons
& Danielson, 1924.
Garrard, Charles G., comp. The Acts and Ordinances
of the Legislative Council of the Straits
Settlements: From the 1st April 1867 to
the 7th March 1898. London: Eyre and
Spottiswoode, 1898.

Gimlette, John D. "Notes on a Case of Amok," *Journal of Tropical Medicine* 4 (June 15, 1901): 195-99.

Gimlette, John D. *A Dictionary of Malayan Medicine.* London: Oxford University Press, 1939.

Griffiths, Percival. *The British Impact on India* London: McDonald, 1952.

Gullick, J. M. *Indigenous Political Systems of Western Malaya.* London: Athlone Press, 1958.

Gullick, J. M. *Malaya.* New York: Praeger, 1963.

Gusfield, Joseph R. "Tradition and Modernity: Misplaced Polarities in the Study of Social Change," *American Journal of Sociology* 72 (1966): 351-62.

Haar, B. ter. "Western Influence on the Law for the Native Population." In *The Effect of Western Influence on Native Civilizations in the Malay Archipelago,* pp. 158-70. Edited by B. Schrieke. Batavia: G. Kolff & Co., 1929.

Hakluyt Society. "A Description of the Coasts of East Africa and Malabar in the Beginning of the 16th Century." In *Barbosa,* pagination unknown. London: Hakluyt Society, 1866. Cited by Henry Yule and A. C. Burnell, eds., *Hobson-Jobson,* p. 20. New ed. Edited by William Crooke. London: John Murray, 1903.

_____. *Peter Floris: His Voyage to the East Indies in the Globe 1611-1615.* London: Hakluyt Society, 1934.

_____. "The Travels of Nicolo Conti in the East in the Early Part of the Fifteenth Century." In *India in the Fifteenth Century.* London: Hakluyt Society, 1857.

_____. *The Travels of Pietro Della Valle in India 1650-53.* London: Hakluyt Society, 1892.

_____. *The Voyage of Sir Henry Middleton to the Moluccas 1604-1606.* London: Hakluyt Society, 1943.

Hall, D. G. E. *A History of South-East Asia.* 2d ed. London: Macmillan, 1964.

Hamid, Wan A. "Religion and Culture of the Modern Malay." In *Malaysia,* pp. 179-189. Edited by Wang Gungwu. London: Pall Mall Press, 1964.

Hartog, J. "The Intervention System for Mental and Social Deviants in Malaysia," *Social Science and Medicine* 6 (1972): 211-20.

Hickson, Sydney J. *A Naturalist in North Celebes.* London: John Murray, 1889.

Hill, Beverley. "An Investigation into Running Amok in Sarawak, Malaysia." B. A. Thesis, Brunel College, University of London, 1970.

Josselin de Jong, P. E. de. "The Rise and Decline of a National Hero," Journal Malayan Branch Royal Asiatic Society 38 (December 1965): 140-55.

Keith, Agnes Newton. Land Below the Wind. Boston: Little, Brown & Co., 1944.

Kennedy, J. A History of Malaya, A.D. 1400-1959. London: Macmillan, 1962.

Kiev, Ari. "Transcultural Psychiatry: Research Problems and Perspectives." In Changing Perspectives in Mental Illness, pp. 106-27. Edited by Stanley C. Plog and Robert B. Edgerton. New York: Holt, Rinehart & Winston, 1969.

Kroef, J. M. van der. Indonesian Social Evolution. Amsterdam: C. P. J. Van der Peet, 1958.

Langness, L. L. "Hysterical Psychosis in the New Guinea Highlands: a Bena Bena Example?" Psychiatry 28 (1965): 258-77.

Lemert, Edwin M. Human Deviance, Social Problems, and Social Control. Englewood Cliffs, N.J.: Prentice-Hall, 1967.

Lenski, Gerhard. Human Societies: A Macrolevel Introduction to Sociology. New York: McGraw-Hill, 1970.

Lerner, Daniel. The Passing of Traditional Society. Glencoe, Ill.: Free Press, 1958.

Lin, Tsung-yi. "Historical Survey of Psychiatric Epidemiology in Asia," Mental Hygiene 47 (1963): 351-59.

Linton, Ralph D. Culture and Mental Disorders. Springfield, Ill.: Charles C. Thomas, 1956.

Logan, J. R. "Malay Amoks and Piracies," Journal of the Indian Archipelago 3 (July 1849): 463-67.

Logan, William. Malabar. 2 vols. 1887; reprint ed., Madras: Government Press, 1951.

Low, Hugh. Sarawak; Its Inhabitants and Productions. London: Richard Bentley, 1848.

Marsden, William. A Dictionary of the Malayan Language. London: Cox and Baylis, 1812.

_____. The History of Sumatra. London: 1811, 3d ed.; reprint ed., Kuala Lumpur: Oxford University Press, 1966.

Maxwell, William G., comp. The Laws of Perak, from the 11th September 1877 to the 31st December 1903. 3 vols. Kuala Lumpur: 1907.

McNair, John Frederick A. Perak and the Malays, reprint ed., Kuala Lumpur: Oxford University Press, 1972.

Metzger, Emil. "Einiges über Amok und Mataglap," Illustrirte Zeitschrift für Länder- und Völkerkunde 52 (1887): 107-23.

Miller, Harry. A Short History of Malaysia. New York: Praeger, 1966.

Moorhead, Francis J. A History of Malaya. 2 vols. Kuala Lumpur: Longmans of Malaya, 1963.

Murphy, Jane M. and Leighton, Alexander H., eds. Approaches to Cross-Cultural Psychiatry. Ithaca, N.Y.: Cornell University Press, 1965.

Newbold, T. J. British Settlements in the Straits of Malacca. 2 vols. London: John Murray, 1839.

Newman, Philip L. "'Wild Man' Behavior in a New Guinea Highlands Community," American Anthropologist 66 (February 1964): 1-19.

Nieuhoff, John. "Mr. John Nieuhoff's Remarkable Voyages and Travels into Brazil, and the Best Parts of the East-Indies," in A Collection of Voyages and Travels. Edited by John Churchill. London: 1704.

Opler, Marvin K. Culture and Social Psychiatry. New York: Atherton Press, 1967.

Ovington, John. A Voyage to Surat in the Year 1689. London: Oxford University Press, 1929.

Oxley, T. "Malay Amoks," Journal of the Indian Archipelago 3 (August 1849): 532-33.

Parsons, Talcott. Societies: Evolutionary and Comparative Perspectives. Englewood Cliffs, N.J.: Prentice-Hall, 1966.

_____. The System of Modern Societies. Englewood Cliffs, N.J.: Prentice-Hall, 1971.

Perak Government Gazette. 4 (March 13, 1891): 131-33.

Phillips, Leslie and Draguns, Juris. "Some Issues in Intercultural Research on Psychopathology." In Mental Health Research in Asia and the Pacific, pp. 21-32. Edited by William Caudill and Tsung-yi Lin. Honolulu: East-West Center Press, 1969.

Pires, Tomé. Suma Oriental, trans. Armando Cortesao. London: Hakluyt Society, 1944. Cited by John Bastin and Robin Winks, eds., Malaysia: Selected Historical Readings. Kuala Lumpur: Oxford University Press, 1966.

Plog, Stanley C. and Edgerton, Robert B., eds. Changing Perspectives in Mental Illness. New York: Holt, Rinehart & Winston, 1969.

Protected Malay States: Annual Reports. London: Eyre & Spottiswoode, 1890.

Radin, Paul. Indians of South America. Garden City, N.Y.: Doubleday, 1946.

Raffles, Lady Sophia. Memoir of the Life and Public Service of Sir Thomas Stamford Raffles. London: James Duncan, 1835.

Raffles, Sir Thomas Stamford. The History of Java. 2 vols. 1817; reprint ed., Kuala Lumpur: Oxford University Press, 1965.

Rasche, Chr. "Ueber die Amok-Kranheit der Malayen," Neurologisches Centralblatt 14 (October 1895): 856-59.

Rassers, W. H. "On the Javanese Kris," Bijdragen tot de Taal-, Land- en Volkenkunde van Nederlandsch-Indie. 99 (1940): 501-83.

Rathborne, Ambrose B. Camping and Tramping in Malaya. London: Swan Sonnenschein & Co., 1898.

Reay, Marie. "Mushrooms and Collective Hysteria," Australian Territories 5 (January 1965): 18-28.

_____. "Mushroom Madness in the New Guinea Highlands," Oceania 31 (1960): 135-39.

Resink, G. J. Indonesia's History Between the Myths. The Hague: W. van Hoeve, 1968.

Resner, Gerald and Hartog, Joseph. "Concepts and Terminology of Mental Disorder Among Malays," Journal of Cross-Cultural Psychology 1 (December, 1970): 369-81.

Roff, William R. The Origins of Malay Nationalism. New Haven: Yale University Press, 1967.

Rosen, George. Madness in Society: Chapters in the Historical Sociology of Mental Illness. Chicago: University of Chicago Press, 1968.

Roth, Henry Ling. The Natives of Sarawak and British North Borneo. London: Trustlove & Hanson, 1896. Cited by Beverly Hill, "An Investigation into Running Amok in Sarawak, Malaysia." B.A. Thesis, Brunel College, University of London, 1970.

Sadka, Emily. The Protected Malay States 1874-1895. Kuala Lumpur: University of Malaya Press, 1968.

Scheube, B. Die Krankheiten Der Warmen Länder. 3d ed. Jena: Verslag von Gustav Fischer, 1903.

Schnitger, F. M. Forgotten Kingdoms in Sumatra. London: E. J. Brill, 1964.

Schoute, Dirk. Occidental Therapeutics in the Netherlands East Indies During Three Centuries of Netherlands Settlement (1600-1900). Batavia: Netherlands Indian Public Health Service, 1937.

176

Schrieke, B., ed. <u>The Effect of Western Influence on Native Civilizations in the Malay Archipelago</u>. Batavia: G. Kolff & Co., 1929.
_____. <u>Indonesian Sociological Studies</u>. The Hague: W. van Hoeve, 1957.
Schulzen, Walter. <u>Ost-Indische Reise-Beschreibung</u>. German edition. Amsterdam: 1676. Cited in Yule and Burnell, <u>Hobson-Jobson</u>.
Sellin, Thorsten. <u>Culture Conflict and Crime</u>. New York: Social Science Research Council, 1938.
Sheppard, Mervyn C. <u>The Adventures of Hang Tuah</u>. Singapore: Eastern Universities Press, 1960.
Smith, Alfred G. "Bibliography of Koro, Amok, and Latah." 1957. (Mimeographed.)
Song ong Siang. <u>One Hundred Years' History of the Chinese in Malaya</u>. Singapore: 1922; reprint ed., Singapore: University of Malaya Press, 1967.
Stavorinus, Johan Splinter. <u>Voyages to the East Indies</u>. 1798; reprint ed., London: Dawsons of Pall Mall, 1969.
Steinberg, David J., ed. <u>In Search of Southeast Asia</u>. New York: Praeger, 1971.
Steinmetz, S. R. "Suicide Among Primitive Peoples," <u>American Anthropologist</u> 7 (January 1894): 53-60.
<u>Straits Settlements: Annual Departmental Reports</u>. Singapore: Government Printing Office, for the years 1899, 1900, 1908, 1909, 1912, 1918.
Swettenham, Sir Frank A. <u>The Real Malay</u>. London: John Lane, The Bodley Head, 1900.
_____. <u>Malay Sketches</u>. London: John Lane, the Bodley Head, 1903.
_____. <u>British Malaya</u>. London: 1907; new ed., London: 1948.
Tarling, Nicholas. <u>A Concise History of Southeast Asia</u>. New York: Praeger, 1966.
Ten Have, J. J. <u>Oost en West</u>. 's-Gravenhage: Joh. Ykema, 1910.
Thio, Alex. "Class Bias in the Sociology of Deviance," <u>American Sociologist</u> 8 (February 1973): 1-12.
Traub, Stuart H. and Little, Craig B., eds. <u>Theories of Deviance</u>. Itasca, Ill.: F. E. Peacock, 1975.
Tregonning, K. G. <u>Home Port Singapore: A History of Straits Steamship Company Limited, 1890-1965</u>. Singapore: Oxford University Press, 1967.
Tsung-yi Lin. "Historical Survey of Psychiatric Epidemiology in Asia," <u>Mental Hygiene</u> 47 (July 1963): 351-59.

Van der Burg, C. L. De Geneesheer in Nederlandsch-
Indië. 2 vols. Batavia: Ernst & Co., 1887.
Van Loon, F. H. "Acute Confusional Insanity in the
Dutch East Indies," Mededeelingen van den
Burgerlijken Geneeskundigen Dienst in
Nederlansch-Indie pt. 4 (1922): 200-220.
_____. "Amok and Lattah," Journal of Abnormal
Psychology 21 (1927): 434-44.
_____. "Protopathic-Instinctive Phenomena in
Normal and Pathological Malay Life," British
Journal of Medical Psychology 8 (1928): 264-
76.
Van Wulfften-Palthe, P. M. "Amok," Nederlandsch
Tijdschrift voor Geneeskunde 77 (1933): 983-
91.
_____. "Amuck or Amok." In A Clinical Textbook
of Tropical Medicine, pp. 529-531. Edited by
Cornelius D. de Langen and A. Lichtenstein.
Batavia: G. Kolff & Co., 1936.
Vlekke, Bernard H. M. Nusantara: A History of
Indonesia. Rev. ed. The Hague: W. van Hoeve,
1960.
Voules, A. B., comp. The Laws of the Federated
Malay States: 1877-1920. London: Hazell,
Watson & Viney, 1921.
Wallace, A. F. C. "Culture Change and Mental
Illness." In Changing Perspectives in Mental
Illness, pp. 75-87. Edited by Stanley C. Plog
and Robert B. Edgerton. New York: Holt
Rinehart & Winston, 1969.
Wallace, Alfred Russel. The Malay Archipelago. New
York: Harper & Brothers, 1869.
Wheeler, L. Richmond. The Modern Malay. London:
George Allen & Unwin, 1928.
Wilkinson, R. J. "Malay Law." In Papers on Malay
Subjects, 1st Series, Law I, pp. 1-68. Edited
by R. J. Wilkinson. Kuala Lumpur: F.M.S.
Government Press, 1908.
Winstedt, Sir Richard. A History of Malaya. Rev.
and enl. ed. Singapore: 1962.
_____. The Malays: A Cultural History. 6th ed.
London: Routledge & Kegan Paul, 1961.
Wissler, Clark. "Societies and Ceremonial
Associations in the Oyala Division of the
Teton-Hakotu," Anthropological Papers of the
American Museum of Natural History vol. 11,
part 1 (1912). Cited by Hill, "An Investi-
gation into Running Amok in Sarawak,
Malaysia," p. 37.
Wolfgang, Marvin E. "Suicide by Means of Victim-
Precipitated Homicide," Journal of Clinical

and Experimental Psychopathology and Quarterly Review of Psychiatry and Neurology 20 (December 1959): 335-49.

Woolley, G. C. "The Malay Keris, Its Origin and Development," Journal Malayan Branch Royal Asiatic Society. 20, part 1 (1947): 60-104.

Yap, Pow Meng. "The Culture-bound Reactive Syndromes." In Mental Health Research in Asia and the Pacific, pp. 33-53. Edited by William Caudill and Tsung-yi Lin. Honolulu: East-West Center Press, 1969.

_____. "Mental Diseases Peculiar to Certain Cultures: A Survey of Comparative Psychiatry," Journal of Mental Science 97 (April 1951): 313-27.

Yule, Henry and Burnell, A. C. Hobson-Jobson. New ed. Edited by William Crooke. London: John Murray, 1903.

Zaguirre, J. C. "Amuck," Journal of the Philippine Federation of Private Medical Practitioners 6 (1957): 1138-49.

Zilboorg, Gregory. "Suicide Among Civilized and Primitive Races," American Journal of Psychiatry 92 (May 1936): 1347-69.

Zwieg, Stefan. The Royal Game; Amok; Letter from an Unknown Woman. Trans. Eden Paul and Cedar Paul. New York: Viking Press, 1944.

ISBN Prefix 0-89680-
Africa Series

25. Kircherr, Eugene C. ABBYSSINIA TO ZIMBABWE: A Guide to the Political Units of Africa in the Period 1947-1978. 1979. 3rd ed. 80pp.
   100-4 $ 8.00*

27. Fadiman, Jeffrey A. MOUNTAIN WARRIORS: The Pre-Colonial Meru of Mt. Kenya. 1976. 82pp.
   060-1 $ 4.75*

36. Fadiman, Jeffrey A. THE MOMENT OF CONQUEST: Meru, Kenya, 1907. 1979. 70pp.
   081-4 $ 5.50*

37. Wright, Donald R. ORAL TRADITIONS FROM THE GAMBIA: Volume I, Mandinka Griots. 1979. 176pp.
   083-0 $12.00*

38. Wright, Donald R. ORAL TRADITIONS FROM THE GAMBIA: Volume II, Family Elders. 1980. 200pp.
   084-9 $15.00*

39. Reining, Priscilla. CHALLENGING DESERTIFICA-TION IN WEST AFRICA: Insights from Landsat into Carrying Capacity, Cultivation and Settlement Site Identification in Upper Volta and Niger. 1979. 180pp., illus.
   102-0 $12.00*

41. Lindfors, Bernth. MAZUNGUMZO: Interviews with East African Writers, Publishers, Editors, and Scholars. 1981. 179pp.
   108-X $13.00*

42. Spear, Thomas J. TRADITIONS OF ORIGIN AND THEIR INTERPRETATION: The Mijikenda of Kenya. 1982. xii, 163pp.
   109-8 $13.50*

43. Harik, Elsa M. and Donald G. Schilling. THE POLITICS OF EDUCATION IN COLONIAL ALGERIA AND KENYA. 1984. 102pp.
   117-9 $11.50*

44. Smith, Daniel R. THE INFLUENCE OF THE FABIAN COLONIAL BUREAU ON THE INDEPENDENCE MOVEMENT IN TANGANYIKA. 1985. x, 98pp.
   125-X $ 9.00*

45. Keto, C. Tsehloane. AMERICAN-SOUTH AFRICAN RELATIONS 1784-1980: Review and Select Bibliography. 1985. 159pp.
128-4 $11.00*

46. Burness, Don, and Mary-Lou Burness, ed. WANASEMA: Conversations with African Writers. 1985. 95pp.
129-2 $ 9.00*

47. Switzer, Les. MEDIA AND DEPENDENCY IN SOUTH AFRICA: A Case Study of the Press and the Ciskei "Homeland". 1985. 80pp.
130-6   9.00*

48. Heggoy, Alf Andrew. THE FRENCH CONQUEST OF ALGIERS, 1830: An Algerian Oral Tradition. 1986. 101pp.
131-4 $ 9.00*

49. Hart, Ursula Kingsmill. TWO LADIES OF COLONIAL ALGERIA: The Lives and Times of Aurelie Picard and Isabelle Eberhardt. 1987. 156pp.
143-8 $9.00*

Latin America Series

1. Frei, Eduardo M. THE MANDATE OF HISTORY AND CHILE'S FUTURE. Tr. by Miguel d'Escoto. Intro. by Thomas Walker. 1977. 79pp.
066-0 $ 8.00*

4. Martz, Mary Jeanne Reid. THE CENTRAL AMERICAN SOCCER WAR: Historical Patterns and Internal Dynamics of OAS Settlement Procedures. 1979. 118pp.
077-6 $ 8.00*

5. Wiarda, Howard J. CRITICAL ELECTIONS AND CRITICAL COUPS: State, Society, and the Military in the Processes of Latin American Development. 1979. 83pp.
082-2 $ 7.00*

6. Dietz, Henry A., and Richard Moore. POLITICAL PARTICIPATION IN A NON-ELECTORAL SETTING: The Urban Poor in Lima, Peru. 1979. viii, 102pp.
085-7 $ 9.00*

7. Hopgood, James F.   SETTLERS OF BAJAVISTA:
    Social and Economic Adaptation in a Mexican
    Squatter Settlement.   1979.   xii, 145pp.
    101-2 $11.00*

8. Clayton, Lawrence A.   CAULKERS AND CARPENTERS
    IN A NEW WORLD: The Shipyards of Colonial
    Guayaquil.   1980.   189pp., illus.
    103-9 $15.00*

9. Tata, Robert J.   STRUCTURAL CHANGES IN PUERTO
    RICO'S ECONOMY: 1947-1976.   1981.   xiv, 104pp.
    107-1 $11.75*

10. McCreery, David.   DEVELOPMENT AND THE STATE IN
    REFORMA GUATEMALA, 1871-1885.   1983.   viii,
    120pp.
    113-6 $ 8.50*

11. O'Shaughnessy, Laura N., and Louis H. Serra.
    CHURCH AND REVOLUTION IN NICARAGUA.   1986.
    118pp.
    126-8 $11.00*

12. Wallace, Brian.   OWNERSHIP AND DEVELOPMENT: A
    Comparison of Domestic and Foreign Investment
    in Columbian Manufacturing.   1987. 186pp.
    145-4 $12.00*

13. Henderson, James D.   CONSERVATIVE THOUGHT IN
    LATIN AMERICA: The Ideas of Laureano Gomez.
    1988.   150pp.
    148-9 $11.00*

14. Summ, G. Harvey, and Tom Kelly.   THE GOOD
    NEIGHBORS: America, Panama, and the 1977 Canal
    Treaties.   1988.   135pp.
    149-7 $11.00*

Southeast Asia Series

31. Nash, Manning.   PEASANT CITIZENS: Politics,
    Religion, and Modernization in Kelantan,
    Malaysia.   1974.   181pp.
    018-0 $12.00*

38. Bailey, Conner.   BROKER, MEDIATOR, PATRON, AND
    KINSMAN: An Historical Analysis of Key Leader-
    ship Roles in a Rural Malaysian District.
    1976.   79pp.
    024-5 $7.00*

40. Van der Veur, Paul W. FREEMASONRY IN INDONESIA FROM RADERMACHER TO SOEKANTO, 1762-1961. 1976. 37pp.
026-1 $4.00*

43. Marlay, Ross. POLLUTION AND POLITICS IN THE PHILIPPINES. 1977. 121pp.
029-6 $7.00*

44. Collier, William L., et al. INCOME, EMPLOYMENT AND FOOD SYSTEMS IN JAVANESE COASTAL VILLAGES. 1977. 160pp.
031-8 $10.00*

45. Chew, Sock Foon and MacDougall, John A. FOREVER PLURAL: The Perception and Practice of Inter-Communal Marriage in Singapore. 1977. 61pp.
030-X $6.00*

47. Wessing, Robert. COSMOLOGY AND SOCIAL BEHAVIOR IN A WEST JAVANESE SETTLEMENT. 1978. 200pp.
072-5 $12.00*

48. Willer, Thomas F., ed. SOUTHEAST ASIAN REFER- ENCES IN THE BRITISH PARLIAMENTARY PAPERS, 1801-1972/73: An Index. 1978. 110pp.
033-4 $ 8.50*

49. Durrenberger, E. Paul. AGRICULTURAL PRODUCTION AND HOUSEHOLD BUDGETS IN A SHAN PEASANT VILLAGE IN NORTHWESTERN THAILAND: A Quantitative Description. 1978. 142pp.
071-7 $9.50*

50. Echauz, Robustiano. SKETCHES OF THE ISLAND OF NEGROS. 1978. 174pp.
070-9 $10.00*

51. Krannich, Ronald L. MAYORS AND MANAGERS IN THAILAND: The Struggle for Political Life in Administrative Settings. 1978. 139pp.
073-3 $ 9.00*

54. Ayal, Eliezar B., ed. THE STUDY OF THAILAND: Analyses of Knowledge, Approaches, and Pros- pects in Anthropology, Art History, Economics, History and Political Science. 1979. 257pp.
079-2 $13.50*

56. Duiker, William J. VIETNAM SINCE THE FALL OF SAIGON. Second edition, revised and enlarged. 1986. 281pp.
133-0 $12.00*

57. Siregar, Susan Rodgers. ADAT, ISLAM, AND
CHRISTIANITY IN A BATAK HOMELAND. 1981.
108pp.
110-1 $10.00*

58. Van Esterik, Penny. COGNITION AND DESIGN
PRODUCTION IN BAN CHIANG POTTERY. 1981. 90pp.
078-4 $12.00*

59. Foster, Brian L. COMMERCE AND ETHNIC DIFFER-
ENCES: The Case of the Mons in Thailand.
1982. x, 93pp.
112-8 $10.00*

60. Frederick, William H., and John H. McGlynn.
REFLECTIONS ON REBELLION: Stories from the
Indonesian Upheavals of 1948 and 1965. 1983.
vi, 168pp.
111-X $ 9.00*

61. Cady, John F. CONTACTS WITH BURMA, 1935-1949:
A Personal Account. 1983. x, 117pp.
114-4 $ 9.00*

62. Kipp, Rita Smith, and Richard D. Kipp, eds.
BEYOND SAMOSIR: Recent Studies of the Batak
Peoples of Sumatra. 1983. viii, 155pp.
115-2 $ 9.00*

63. Carstens, Sharon, ed. CULTURAL IDENTITY IN
NORTHERN PENINSULAR MALAYSIA. 1986. 91pp.
116-0 $ 9.00*

64. Dardjowidjojo, Soenjono. VOCABULARY BUILDING
IN INDONESIAN: An Advanced Reader. 1984.
xviii, 256pp.
118-7 $26.00*

65. Errington, J. Joseph. LANGUAGE AND SOCIAL
CHANGE IN JAVA: Linguistic Reflexes of Modernization in a Traditional Royal Polity. 1985.
xiv, 198pp.
120-9 $12.00*

66. Binh, Tran Tu. THE RED EARTH: A Vietnamese
Memoir of Life on a Colonial Rubber Plantation.
Tr. by John Spragens. Ed. by David Marr.
1985. xii, 98pp.
119-5 $ 9.00*

67. Pane, Armijn. SHACKLES. Tr. by John McGlynn.
Intro. by William H. Frederick. 1985. xvi,
108pp.
122-5 $ 9.00*

68. Syukri, Ibrahim. HISTORY OF THE MALAY KINGDOM OF PATANI. Tr. by Conner Bailey and John N. Miksic. 1985. xx, 98pp.
123-3 $10.50*

69. Keeler, Ward. JAVANESE: A Cultural Approach. 1984. xxxvi, 523pp.
121-7 $18.00*

70. Wilson, Constance M., and Lucien M. Hanks. BURMA-THAILAND FRONTIER OVERSIXTEEN DECADES: Three Descriptive Documents. 1985. x, 128pp.
124-1 $10.50*

71. Thomas, Lynn L., and Franz von Benda-Beckmann, eds. CHANGE AND CONTINUITY IN MINANGKABAU: Local, Regional, and Historical Perspectives on West Sumatra. 1986. 363pp.
127-6 $14.00*

72. Reid, Anthony, and Oki Akira, eds. THE JAPANESE EXPERIENCE IN INDONESIA: Selected Memoirs of 1942-1945. 1986. 411pp., 20 illus.
132-2 $18.00*

73. Smirenskaia, Ahanna D. PEASANTS IN ASIA: Social Consciousness and Social Struggle. Tr. by Michael J. Buckley. 1987. 248pp.
134-9 $12.50

74. McArthur, M.S.H. REPORT ON BRUNEI IN 1904. Ed. by A.V.M. Horton. 1987. 304pp.
135-7 $13.50

75. Lockard, Craig Alan. FROM KAMPUNG TO CITY. A Social History of Kuching Malaysia 1820-1970. 1987. 311pp.
136-5 $14.00*

76. McGinn, Richard. STUDIES IN AUSTRONESIAN LINGUISTICS. 1988. 492pp.
137-3 $18.50*

78. Chew, Sock Foon. ETHNICITY AND NATIONALITY IN SINGAPORE. 1987. 229pp.
139-X $12.50*

79. Walton, Susan Pratt. MODE IN JAVANESE MUSIC. 1987. 279pp.
144-6 $12.00*

80. Nguyen Anh Tuan. SOUTH VIETNAM TRIAL AND EXPERIENCE: A Challenge for Development. 1987. 482pp.
141-1 $15.00*

81. Van der Veur, Paul W., ed. TOWARD A GLORIOUS INDONESIA: Reminiscences and Observations of Dr. Soetomo. 1987. 367pp.
142-X $13.50*

ORDERING INFORMATION

Orders for titles in the Monographs in International Studies series should be placed through the Ohio University Press/Scott Quadrangle/Athens, Ohio 45701-2979. Individuals must remit pre-payment via check, VISA, MasterCard, CHOICE, or American Express. Individuals ordering from the United Kingdom, Continental Europe, Middle East, and Africa should order through Academic and University Publishers Group, 1 Gower Street, London WC1E 6HA, England. Other individuals ordering from outside of the U.S., please remit in U.S. funds by either International Money Order or check drawn on a U.S. bank. Postage and handling is $2.00 for the first book and $.50 for each additional book. Prices and availability are subject to change without notice.

DATE DUE

MAR 0 1 1989			
GAYLORD			PRINTED IN U.S.A.